PROBLEM CHILD

KHALID N. MUMIN

LEADING STUDENTS LIVING IN POVERTY
TOWARDS INFINITE POSSIBILITIES OF SUCCESS

ISBN: 978-1-7324781-4-5

Editing: Wandah Gibbs, Ed. D.

Cover Art: Damian Brown

Printed in the United States

WGW Publishing Inc., Rochester, NY

...For my late mother, Khadijah Mu'Min and my father William Bey, who as young parents exemplified the greatest strength, perseverance, patience, and LOVE in raising a son from infancy to reaching infinite possibilities of success. It takes a village to raise a child, and they were the leaders of the village for many young people to follow. They taught us to aspire towards greatness...

---THANK YOU. THANK YOU. THANK YOU!

William Bey, Khadijah Mu'Min, Khalid Mumin

FOREWARD|

By Robert L. Green, Ph.D., Distinguished Professor Emeritus, Michigan State University, East Lansing, Michigan

Having been in education for the better part of my life, it remains one of my goals to mentor and support educators who strive to improve educational outcomes for all youth. My passion for equity has been stoked by the struggles we've overcome and the journey we have yet to complete.

I joined the staff of the Southern Christian Leadership Conference (SCLC) in 1965 where Dr. Martin Luther King Jr. appointed me National Education Director. I later became the Director of the Center for Urban Affairs at Michigan State University and was the National Consultant to the NAACP on desegregation. I served as an expert witness in more than 20 school desegregation cases in the 5th circuit court.

Over the past 50 years, I have worked directly with hundreds of school district superintendents. I have observed how their educational leadership, their belief in education, coupled with what they deem important in education, directly influence the districts over which they preside.

Robert L. Green Ph.D., Former National Education Director, Appointed by Dr. Martin Luther King Jr.

I met Khalid Mumin years ago through another renowned educator, Dr. Tony Hicks. At the time, Khalid was Superintendent of Schools at Caroline County Public Schools, in Denton, Maryland. I was impressed by his passion and leadership.

In getting to know him, I became privy to his personal journey which further inspired me to mentor and support him along the way. Although Khalid's mother and father had separated when he was young, they were both in agreement in regards to his upbringing: 1) stay out of trouble, 2) go to school every day, 3) do your homework. Furthermore, when and if he misbehaved, his mother would swiftly send him four blocks down the street to his father's house, to be disciplined.

Khalid listened to the adults in his life; his mom, dad, and a judge. At one point he went before a juvenile court judge to be disciplined for something he had done. The judge said, "Look, your mother has a job, she works hard, and she doesn't have time to take off work to bring you to court. If you come in my courtroom again, you're going to be placed in a boy's home." Khalid listened to the judge, and never went back to court again.

His parents played a role in disciplining him, played a role in making sure he stayed on track, and more importantly, his mother constantly pushed him towards education. She was someone who believed in social justice, and she often talked to him about treating people fairly. Khalid has become an expert in these areas and uses this acquired skillset in his day-to-day operations.

Sports also played a large role in his life. Khalid was an excellent basketball player in high school and in college. He did not however let sports distract him from his academic work. Besides, his mother was always there keeping an eye on him from the shadows to ensure he stayed on track. Khalid mentions an athlete in the book whom I knew very well. He was a close friend of the family and a frequent house guest of mine: – Mr. Arthur Ashe. Though a tremendous tennis player, he was also an honor student while at UCLA. Ashe was a scholar and a gentleman who diplomatically used his platform as a well-known athlete and scholar to promote the value of education.

I distinctly remember being invited to a public event with Khalid one evening, when I overheard a young lady challenging the event planner about the seating arrangements. She was firm, direct, yet articulate and when she'd finished pleading her case, she had calmly acquired the seat she'd asked for. Khalid noticed the exchange, and eventually approached the young woman in question. "Hi, do you remember me?" He asked. "Yes! You were my high school teacher. You're the one who taught me how to go about challenging situations in a positive manner. I now do that whenever necessary and it works!" You see, Khalid uses a holistic approach in education; one that encompasses both soft skills and academic achievement.

Many books have been written about moving from poverty to success, and they often cite education as a vehicle. This book supports that view but also provides a clear pathway for making education palatable and effective for all children. Khalid himself is a man who went through various struggles and pains in life, and yet succeeded. And, why did he succeed? Namely, because he learned to listen to the adults in his life who cared about him, and those who had his best interests at heart.

Problem Child, by Khalid N. Mumin, is a must-read for all teachers and educators as it further emphasizes that education is a powerful force in overcoming poverty. It demonstrates how one can beat the odds through education. It also illustrates how education can then lead us towards a better life, one that reaches much farther than the eradication of poverty. He illustrates how it enables us to raise our children in a more definitive way, allows us to take care of our families, and helps us to help others succeed as well. *Problem Child* presents a dramatic, living example of the power of mentorship in education. Khalid effectively emphasizes the fact that once you've earned your degree, no one can take it from you. It's yours forever.

His life story and work remind me of my own upbringing. My father and mother believed in just what Khalid teaches. Though my father, only made it through 4th grade and my mother through the 6th, their children and grandchildren obtained over 85 degrees between them to include bachelor's, master's degrees, Ph. D.s, and M.D.s. They firmly believed that education is the clear path to a better life and they instilled that in us at every turn.

I got to know Martin Luther King Jr. and his family personally. There is no question in my mind of the importance he placed on education. Khalid Mumin is a living testimony of the power of education, which he clearly outlines in his work and I know beyond the shadow of a doubt that Martin Luther King, Jr. would have endorsed this book.

It is indeed refreshing to see a young man so devoted to educating our youth. As one who has lived it, he believes in the power of mentorship and knows that when someone believes in you, it provides the necessary fuel to propel you forward. Khalid's book is inspiring, refreshing, and long overdue. I, along with many others, am delighted that he is finally sharing his expertise in print...

INTRODUCTION|

I grew up living in poverty in Philadelphia, Pennsylvania "The City of Brotherly Love". It was the 90's where escaping poverty was filled with dreams of becoming a famous athlete, entertainer or artist. And, many of my peers attempted to escape poverty the fast way through illegal activities, thus more often than not, becoming a negative statistic and casualty of poverty. Dropping out of school, homelessness, incarceration, and death were common outcomes where I grew up.

After a brief period of truancy in high school, some delinquency, and the possibility of being incarcerated in a youth detention center, I was scared straight. I slowly began to understand that living in poverty was real, and that I too could easily become a statistic, further perpetuating the cycle.

Following this reality check, I became one of the few children who listened to my elders. I accepted support and mentorship from people who had bigger dreams for me than I did. I eventually allowed them to convince me that education was in fact the vehicle that would lead me out of poverty towards a brand-new world of infinite possibilities and success.

This book examines the historical constructs of youth growing up in poverty and shows how educators with high expectations committed to teaching and leading leads to achievement. It reveals how influential mentorship is one of the major pillars of success. Moreover, great teachers and influential leaders who understand poverty, and who build sustainable relationships with children are a large part of the equation. Maintaining high expectations and believing that defeating poverty is truly a form of social justice in an ever-changing society, serves to motivate children to defeat the odds in beating poverty and all of its ills.

Herein you'll find a three-pronged approach at addressing teaching and leadership for students who grow up in underserved communities. This approach looks at the impact district leaders can have. It also examines how teachers and pedagogues in the classroom, who motivate and guide students and who include student voice in the equation are impacting student outcomes.

Prong one encourages school district leaders to: (1) advocate for policy and funding to address the diverse needs of children, (2) recruitment, hiring and retention of extraordinary teachers, (3) supporting and empowering teachers to deliver instruction with high expectations, (4) commit to making school districts more flexible and efficient, and (5) creating pathways for students to be active participants in their schooling through vison, voice, and completion of attainable goals.

Prong two empowers teachers to: (1) become consummate advocates for the children they serve, (2) take on the challenge to understand poverty, (3) build sustainable relationships, (4) commit to becoming leaders in social justice and equity, and (5) having the confidence to teach with high expectations beyond the scope of standardized testing.

Prong three is designed for students to: (1) understand their importance in schools, in the classroom and beyond, (2) establish their voice, (3) impact school district policy, (4) succeed to high expectations, and (5) have the confidence to graduate and make a positive impact in an ever-changing society.

This book describes and outlines the infinite possibilities in educating students from underserved communities plagued by poverty. This is by no means a *silver bullet* that addresses everything poverty related where education is concerned. However, it can be a valuable resource and toolkit in further addressing the multifaceted issues poverty brings with it into the classroom. It sets forth ideas so leaders can lead, teachers can teach, and whereby students can learn to defeat historical odds.

TABLE OF CONTENTS|

CHAPTER ONE| MY BACKGROUND

The Road Not Taken
By Robert Frost

Two roads diverged in a yellow wood,
And sorry I could not travel both
And be one traveler, long I stood
And looked down one as far as I could
To where it bent in the undergrowth;

Then took the other, as just as fair,
And having perhaps the better claim,
Because it was grassy and wanted wear;
Though as for that the passing there
Had worn them really about the same,

And both that morning equally lay
In leaves no step had trodden black.
Oh, I kept the first for another day!
Yet knowing how way leads on to way,
I doubted if I should ever come back.

I shall be telling this with a sigh
Somewhere ages and ages hence:
Two roads diverged in a wood, and I—
I took the one less traveled by,
And that has made all the difference.

The Road|

I was born in 1972 to two extraordinary parents. Both my mother, Khadijah, and my father, William, were young when the Civil Rights Movement began. My mom was born and raised in Wilmington, North Carolina, and my father in Philadelphia, Pennsylvania. Though they were from two different areas of the country, they were connected with one mindset; equity, equal representation, access to opportunity, and empowerment. When my mother was just nine years old, my maternal grandmother passed away. My mom then had to take on the role of head of household raising her three sisters, while my grandfather drove trucks throughout the United States. At the age of 17, my mother and my grandfather moved to Philadelphia.

Within a year, my mom met Mr. Fletcher. He was 10 years older than her and was a hustler and savvy businessman. Urban legend in my family has it that Mr. Fletcher courted my mom by lavishing her with fancy gifts; mink coats, diamonds, and fancy shoes. Meanwhile he used his business savvy to win my grandfather's approval for marriage. I remember my grandfather often referred to Mr. Fletcher as a man with nice shoes and lots of money, which is why he'd felt comfortable supporting Mr. Fletcher's advances to marry my mom. They had a short courtship then my sister was born in the summer of 1968.
The newlyweds were madly in love, but their relationship was a volatile one filled with arguments and

fights. One day, while the two of them were seated in a bar, a young lady walked up to them and said to Mr. Fletcher with a sassy drawl, "hey daddy, how come you don't talk to momma no more?" Story has it, Mr. Fletcher responded with: "bitch don't you see I'm here with my wife!" Then apparently Mr. Fletcher and Mom delivered a beat down to the potential homewrecker. In 1972, while Mom and Mr. Fletcher were on again, off again in their marriage, my mom, while sitting for an admissions competency exam at Temple University, met a young man named William. My mother was attempting to cheat off of my father's exam but could not see around his broad shoulders. Aware of what she was trying to do, he moved his exam into clearer view. After the exam was over, my father told her that he saw her attempts at cheating, and wanted to help. He then told her that it had not been necessary to cheat as he'd seen her answers and they were correct...

William's educational prowess, love of philosophy and history were an instant turn on for my mom. It didn't hurt that my father at 6'5" was not only tall, dark, and handsome but he was also a tremendous swimmer, who had qualified for the Olympic trials. He was also a hustler but with an academic mind, and even though he was from the North he had the mindset of a freedom fighter.

My father was born in North Philadelphia in a two-parent household and had three siblings. My paternal grandmother was a music teacher in the School District of Philadelphia, and my grandfather was an editor for the now defunct Philadelphia Bulletin daily newspaper. When my father was nine years old, he lost his father in a car accident. My grandfather was struck and killed instantly as he stepped off the curb into traffic on Broad Street while reading the newspaper. This event changed my father's life. He became the man of the house and sought answers on how to become a man in the streets of North Philadelphia. Somehow however, my father maintained a balance between being a hustler and an intellectual. He was quick to engage in neighborhood gang wars one minute, then debating with friends about the ills of American culture the next. He liked to emphasize the words of Sam Cooke's song, *A Change Gonna Come.*

In 1964, my father was one of the children who joined the adults in the riots, burning down Columbia Avenue near Temple University's campus. It was a race riot; African Americans were upset with police brutality, racism, and the lack of Black empowerment. They burned buildings on Columbia Avenue except the Black Nationalists' center which still exists today, even in its decrepit, aged form.

Columbia Avenue was renamed Cecil B. Moore Avenue after Cecil Bassett Moore, a Philadelphia lawyer and civil rights activist who led the fight to integrate Girard College. He was president of the local NAACP, and a member of Philadelphia's City Council.

What was born out of the renaming of the avenue was that Black citizenry in North Philadelphia felt empowered, liberated, and as if their voices made a difference in the cultural context and development of North Philadelphia. This is where my mother and father united on the same accord as revolutionists fighting the power of the establishment. My father often reminisced about taking the Temple University entrance exam only to prove to himself that he could engage and compete on a college level, even though he had no intention of becoming a student.

In the summer of 1972, while legally separated from Mr. Fletcher, my mother gave birth to me. In the words of Diana Ross, I was a *love child*. This was the apex of my mother and father's relationship, as he gave my mother an ultimatum, which included divorcing her husband and joining the Moorish Science Temple of America. My mother eventually divorced Mr. Fletcher, but she chose to become a Muslim who followed the teachings of The Honorable Elijah Muhammed and later The Honorable Warith Dean Muhammed. Therefore, I was raised in a single parent home. I lived with my mother and sister, while my father lived four blocks away, married with a growing family. I was fortunate that my home life, although nontraditional, was not dysfunctional. I received love in both homes, while practicing Muslim Islam with my mother and Islam defined by the teachings of The Honorable Noble Drew Ali in the Moorish Science Temple of America, when I visited my father.

My Father, William Bey

Khadijah Mu'Min

My Mother, First in her Family to Graduate College

Young Khalid Mumin

I never wanted for anything. My mother kept me well dressed, educated, culturally aware, and competent. I define dysfunctional homes at times as home settings with a combination or confluence of abuse, absent parenting and direction, scarce resources being either poverty or love, and a lack of goal setting for the family. Non-traditional homes include a circle of support, love, direction, and goal setting for the future. A house does not define what a home setting is or can become. Homes include love, whereas dysfunctional homes have an absence of it.

My mother worked three jobs, while attending college to become a registered nurse. My sister excelled in school, and I always received passing grades as a young student through 8th grade. It was during my 9th grade school year that my worlds collided and crashed. I was disappointed that I could not attend my neighborhood school due to the School District of Philadelphia making attempts to diversify schools by sending students to schools outside of their neighborhoods.

Some might say I loved 9th grade so much that I did it twice! The first year outside of my neighborhood was a disaster. Coming from a section of Philadelphia called Logan, I received bus tokens to attend a school in Northeast Philadelphia. I can remember that almost every day, kids from Logan fought with kids from the Northeast just to make it through the doors of the high school. I was never afraid to engage in a fight, because my sister taught me how to "hold my hands." I frequently had to defend myself and the honor of my neighborhood simply to attend school.

One day in November of 1984 things went drastically wrong. While in the school cafeteria, I became surrounded by a group of students from a rival neighborhood. They slapped me in the face multiple times, stole my hat and gold chain. Snatching off hats and chains was not a scheme to make money in the 80's, instead it was a blatant sign of disrespect.

After that incident, I attended school every day with one mission in mind: revenge. This is when I had to learn to balance fighting outside of school to represent my neighborhood while learning in school to appease my family. I was in so much emotional pain as my pride had been damaged. Then, it happened; I saw the thug who'd snatched my belongings, and I immediately unleashed a flurry of punches. I hit him in the head with a metal trash can knocking him unconscious. Needless to say, I was suspended from school for 10 days with a required meeting between my mother, myself, and the principal before I could be reinstated.

I knew the school would be sending a suspension letter to our house, so I simply arrived home early every day after school to check the mail and intercept any suspension letters. On record, I remained out of school for approximately 75 days, though I was only supposed to be serving a 10-day suspension. The readmission could not take place, as my mother never received the letters asking her to meet with the principal.

Meanwhile, I was a truant student masquerading with family as though I was still attending class. Instead I was engaging in risky behaviors during the school day; fighting, stealing, gambling, playing video games, and basketball every day. Then, whenever I'd show up on school property, I'd find myself running from the police as they tried to apprehend me for trespassing. I was locked in a cycle destined to lead me from the schoolhouse to the big house. I became the archetypical example of the school to prison pipeline that currently plagues inner-city youth. **Zero tolerance discipline policies lead to "one size fits all" consequences.**

Requiring every student receive a 10-day suspension for any type of fight in high school is an example of zero tolerance. There is no chance for progressive discipline, where a behavioral, social or emotional assessment can be made by school officials to differentiate disciplinary measures. Perhaps, there could have been a meeting to determine the severity of the disciplinary incident, and restorative practices could have been implemented to steer me back on track. Or, maybe school district personnel, such as a home school visitor, truancy officer or social worker could have visited my home to gain deeper insight into why I had not attended school for two entire marking periods. Unbeknownst to me, as a 9th grade student I had already been labeled a problem child and was on pace to permanent expulsion for simply engaging in one fight and subsequently avoiding school.

I eventually tired of running from the police, was tired of fighting, tired of stealing, and tired of maintaining the facade of being a responsible student. So, I gave up one day and turned myself in to the police on school grounds. This turned out to be a big a mistake. It was now April 1985, and I had not officially been in school since November of 1984. I was immediately arrested, handcuffed, then marched through the cafeteria, so all the students could witness a *thug* being taken down.

I was sad and depressed, because I knew how surprised and disappointed my mother would be. Though I still get emotional when reflecting on this turn of events, I refused to cry back then, because I felt that I was a man and "men don't cry!" I wanted to go out on my feet like a man. I wanted to represent my neighborhood like a man. I wanted to take my consequences "on the chin" like a man. Thus, while being transported to the police precinct, I engaged in banter with the other detainees and police officers *like a man*. A police officer patrolling the room demanded we stop the banter.

Meanwhile, my mother had been contacted and soon arrived at the police station. As a juvenile that made every effort to maintain a balance between education and street life, I was savvy enough (or so I thought), to believe that once my mother arrived, I would be set free and sent home, because after all, I was a juvenile.

Instead, my mother informed me that I would be transported to the Philadelphia Youth Study Center (PYSC) and not being permitted to go home. As tears welled up in her eyes, she asked me if I was being treated fairly and if I needed anything. I simply asked my mom to bring me some sneakers or boots, because I had been arrested while wearing dress shoes, and that would make me an instant target at the PYSC. As our visit concluded and the officer was escorting me back to the holding area, he stopped and gave me a 20 to 30-minute tongue lashing for giving my mother so much grief.

The officer told me I was a major disappointment. After a conversation he'd had with my mother, he realized I had a "Saint" in my corner. He learned I had been given everything I needed as a child, but that I was determined to be a tough guy. He held my attention especially when he said I was risking becoming another Black statistic because of my egregious behavior. When I returned to the holding area the officer told me, "today must be your lucky day." Turns out the other juvenile detainees had already been transported to the PYSC, and juveniles were not permitted to stay detained in a police station for more than 24 hours straight. My mother was asked to return to the precinct to take me home until my court appearance date.

My court appearance was scheduled approximately three weeks after my initial arrest. Those three weeks went by really fast. To this day, I cannot recall what I did, while waiting to appear in court, though I remember isolating myself from family and friends. Everyone was extremely disappointed in the behavior I exhibited. My family and friends' reactions included; tremendous anger, disappointment, ostracization, and counting me out from having a successful future.

At long last the three weeks came to an end and it was my day to appear in court. All the courage I had generated wanting to be a man and take my consequences came to a crashing halt when my name was called to appear. The courtroom holding pen included several people I recognized; friends and foes alike, and some of the very people I had done battle or business with in the streets of Philadelphia. As each of them was called one after the other, I was curious as to why they never resurfaced in the holding cell. Hence, I asked my sister where they'd disappeared to? She told me they were "being sent up," meaning they were being given lengthy sentences in juvenile placement centers.

I immediately ran out of the court holding pen and retreated to a bathroom in an attempt to make a getaway. My mother appeared right behind me and commenced to berate me. She pointed out that if I did not appear before the judge like a man, I was destined to be a failure embarking on a life wrought with incarceration.
I finally appeared in the courtroom. The assistant district superintendent testified on behalf of the school district. He said I was a juvenile delinquent with a criminal history and terrible attendance due to my lengthy suspension and failure to report for

reinstatement to school. He continuously berated me, while my court appointed public defender said nothing. I remember, the assistant district attorney stating that the reason for my demise as a truant student was because I had a deadbeat mother. I responded, by stating it was not my mother's fault that I was truant. She worked every day. I acted as if I was going to school every day, but never made it over the threshold of the school doors, because each day was a battle. Because of neighborhood rivalries I had to fight just to get onto the school grounds. Going to school in the northeast section of Philadelphia, while a resident of Logan, was just not safe, nor did it seem worth it.

The judge called on my mother to provide her side of the story to the court, which she did. She explained how raising me was a challenge while she worked three jobs amidst finalizing her Bachelor's degree in nursing. The judge suddenly realized that my mother worked for the Northwest Center, a safe haven for youth and adults where they learned to gain life skills and receive emotional and social support. The judge stopped immediately and exclaimed that his wife also worked at the Northwest Center. He stopped court, picked up the receiver to a rotary dial phone, and called his wife who was on the Board of Directors at the Northwest Center. Even though the brief conversation he had with his wife seemed like an eternity, I remember he asked her about my mother, my family, and more specifically my negative influence on the family. The judge then hung up the phone and directed me to approach the bench. He said,

"Son, I spoke to my wife about your mother. She is a lovely woman, a Saint, and you are a mess. Your mother does everything for you, and you are slowly but surely becoming a disgrace. She works hard at her job and in her studies, while you are throwing your life away." Everything and everyone in the courtroom paused, as he told me a story:

I vacation each year in Maryland. I have a sailboat and travel the Chesapeake Bay each day. This allows me to get a different look at the world. It's relaxing. It is pure serenity. Each day that I travel, it feels like the world is never ending. I know when I leave for a voyage, I am leaving the stress of the world behind me and when I dock at the end of the day, I am prepared to take on life's challenges with a renewed sense of vigor, goals, and view of society. My suggestion young man is that you find your sailboat in life. Travel far each day. Travel away from the people you accept as your friends. Take a trip, look back at what you left behind, and find your own way, your own sense of serenity. As a matter of fact, you better take my advice, because I am sentencing you to 18-24 months of probation with counseling services at the Northwest Center. You are angry for no reason. You are a mess! If you embrace this challenge, you will become a success story. If you do not embrace this challenge and I have to see you again, you will be sentenced to all 18-24 months at a juvenile facility. This means, if you miss one session of counseling, even the last one, I will sentence you to all 18-24 months. Don't disappoint yourself. Don't disappoint your mother. Good luck.

I was elated; I had escaped jail! So, I strolled through the holding pen with great confidence and bravado. More importantly it was the beginning of my journey towards becoming a responsible son, brother, and student. I created a sailboat in my mind, left the port, and never returned to my peers after I left the dock. As Robert Frost stated in the poem *A Road Not Taken*, "I shall be telling this with a sigh, Somewhere ages and ages hence: Two roads diverged in a wood, and I—I took the one less traveled and that has made all the difference."

Charting a Course|

I left the dock and travelled to another land. The destination was a pathway to success in the educational system. My second chance at graduation included attending my neighborhood high school, where I was safe from rivals as I was able to travel with a large group of like-minded students. We loved the city. We loved our neighborhood, and we made a commitment to become successful by any means necessary. We were athletes, but not jocks. We wanted to defy the odds of becoming playground legend wannabees by working hard on the basketball court and in school. Along this pathway is where my life dramatically changed. I met influential educators that saw the potential in me that I myself couldn't see at the time. Like many students, I had day to day carpe diem goals, but I did not have a consistent plan for college and career readiness or success.

These influential educators and beacons of hope were my school counselor, assistant principal, basketball coach, English teacher and English Department chairperson. These people changed my life! Mrs. Martin, the school counselor ingrained in me weekly that I was college material. Mrs. Horter, the assistant principal constantly reminded me of the effects of failure and statistics that impact young African American boys, who do not complete high school. Coach Evans was a father figure who reinforced the importance of education, discipline, competing, and becoming a responsible man. Mr. Smith enlightened me to the value of not only partaking in school but also striving to become an academic. Dr. Wahl opened the doors to several culturally competent experiences which helped diversify my thinking and mindset. These beacons of light were larger than life and they took the time to mentor and prepare me for success in an ever-changing society.

There's nothing better for an adolescent than working hard and facing life's struggles while prominent adults stand beside you and cheer you on as you travel towards success. In hindsight, the pathway is a marathon and these angels, constantly nourish and cheer for you throughout the race. Consequently, I aimed to please these inspiring adults. They made me feel important. They made me feel like I was a contributor in school. They empowered me to do great things and they supported me as I periodically crashed and burned along the way.

A few epiphanies come to mind that solidified my experience. One day I entered Mr. Smith's English class and quickly realized that he was not present. My mind shifted at the thought of our teacher being absent and a substitute having to take the reins. However, Mr. Smith always carried a heavily worn leather briefcase and I recognized that it was prominently displayed on his desk even in his perceived absence. I was perplexed wondering if he really was absent for the day because Mr. Smith never missed school. He would attend even when he was sick, saddened by a family event, and on snow emergency days. Then it happened!

Mr. Smith suddenly emerged into the classroom dressed in witches clothing while creepy music played in the background. He rushed in as if he was flying on a broom and began to chant, "Double, double toil and trouble; fire burn, and caldron bubble. Double, double toil and trouble; fire burn, and caldron bubble. Double, double toil and trouble, fire burn, and caldron bubble. Double, double toil and trouble; fire burn, and caldron bubble." I was mesmerized by Mr. Smith's antics. His behavior was bizarre while his outfit was spectacular. He stopped and asked, do you know what I am saying? The class responded with a resounding "no!" Mr. Smith then told us that we knew nothing about rap because we had not understood what we'd just heard. He proclaimed that we had just heard rhymes from the best rapper that ever lived: William Shakespeare. Mr. Smith said, "He is better than any rapper you've ever heard, better than Run DMC, better than LL Cool J, better than Public Enemy, and better than Big Daddy Kane."

The class then started following a read along to Macbeth. Each day, we read along to the unabridged version, engaging in the banter of witches, while examining the many complexities of the main character, King Macbeth. Following two weeks of reading, Mr. Smith said that we had just read a classic work. Who would have imagined that inner-city students would read and learn the works of one of the greatest authors in literary history? My confidence as a student was soaring. Mr. Smith had engaged me in challenging work, while referring to my musical literary knowledge and challenging me to learn what children were learning in the suburbs.

This academic success ignited an intrinsic drive to become smarter and more knowledgeable, so I began to read ferociously. I read works from the greats such as Langston Hughes, James Baldwin, and Ralph Waldo Ellison. These authors resonated with me and I was just beginning to understand the importance of being African American; our accomplishments, relevance, and responsibility to achieve academically, thus promoting economic growth and mobility. Specifically, Langston Hughes taught me that jazz was cool echoing originality, culture and class, while reminding me that "I Too Sing America," striving for social justice and equity. James Baldwin reminded me in *The Fire Next Time* that racism was not a new phenomenon but a brazen scar on American history that lives on to this day. Thus, the civil rights movement is ongoing and everlasting. Most importantly, Ralph Ellison spoke to my soul and continues to live within me with his book, *Invisible Man*, as I seek to tell my story to the world in the dark underground and unnoticed.

Succinctly, Mr. Smith fed literary knowledge to me while challenging me to be great and defy the odds. The wonderful educators I learned from expected greatness from each of us. They did not have low academic expectations for me just because I was poor.

Dr. Wahl solidified the experience by providing us with tickets and by absorbing transportation costs for any student interested in watching the works of Shakespeare being performed at Temple University. I immediately jumped at the opportunity to see the work we read in class come to life on the stage.

I knew from this experience that I was destined to become an English teacher. The fire that had been lit in my heart and soul became a driving force. Being held to high expectations is a leadership lesson that has followed me throughout my adult life. Because I graduated from high school with horrendous Scholastic Aptitude Test (SAT) scores, I entered a two-year college.

Following graduation from Junior college, I attended Shippensburg University on an academic and athletic scholarship where I majored in English/Language Arts. While there I was voted captain of the basketball team, and engaged in several civic groups. I graduated with a modest grade point average earning a Bachelor's of Arts and a certification in Secondary English Education.

I then began teaching middle school English, acquired a Master's of Education at Pennsylvania State University and elevated from a teaching position to Dean of Students, then Assistant Principal, followed by Principal. The journey continued as I reached the academic epitome of success by earning a Doctorate of Education from the University of Pennsylvania. I became a Distinguished Alumni Award recipient at Shippensburg University in May 2019. Professionally, I elevated from Principal to Director of Secondary Education followed by Superintendent of Schools.

In spite of all of the aforementioned experiences and successes I often reflect upon how I reached this pinnacle. Was it through sheer luck? Was I provided secret opportunities? Was I handed opportunities because of who I knew? The answer is emphatically no! I was led towards the pathway of success by mentors and supporters who saw the potential in me that I at first could not see for myself. Once I got on track, I lived and worked hard, often seizing the day. My mentors had the wisdom and experience necessary to see a successful future for me, one where I would succeed. They were dream keepers and supporters standing alongside me as I fiercely tackled the journey.

I, Too

By Langston Hughes

I, too, sing America.

I am the darker brother.
They send me to eat in the kitchen
When company comes,
But I laugh,
And eat well,
And grow strong.

Tomorrow,
I'll be at the table
When company comes.
Nobody'll dare
Say to me,
"Eat in the kitchen,"
Then.

Besides,
They'll see how beautiful I am
And be ashamed—

I, too, am America.

I Too|

My mother, father, and powerful educators such as; Mr. Smith, Dr. Wahl, Mrs. Edwards, and Coach Evans motivated me to be all I could be in life and to reach my full potential. They allowed me to dream, explore, take risks, and build academic confidence. Coach Evans took the time to ignite my athletic gifts. I was a 6'3" small forward and captain of the 1989-90 basketball team at Olney High School where I became an honorable mention all-star athlete. I was invited to the 1990 Philadelphia Public Schools All Public Basketball All Star Game, where I led the public league in dunks. As an academic talent and prowess on the basketball court, I was gaining the attention of basketball coaches mostly from small division I and division II programs in the northeast United States. However, I was hit with a buzz saw, when I had to take the Scholastic Aptitude Test (SAT). The Princeton Review defines the SAT as: "An entrance exam used by most colleges and universities to make admissions decisions. It is a multiple-choice, pencil-and-paper test administered by the College Board."

There was information on the examination that I had never seen before in high school. The information was foreign, I was fatigued by the length of the test, and as a result, I failed miserably. My score was in the range of 450-500 out of a total score of 1650. More importantly, I needed to achieve a score of 700 or better to be considered as a scholar-athlete. I was perplexed, upset, and disappointed that my pathway out of the "hood" would be blocked by a test. I could not understand that I was ranked in the top ten percent of my graduating class, had good grades, could play basketball with the best yet could not participate in scholarship opportunities at the collegiate level. The reality sunk in that I was a *Proposition 48* which is an NCAA regulation that stipulates minimum high school grades coupled with standardized test scores that student-athletes must meet in order to participate in college athletic competition.

I was furious that one assessment would be used to determine my potential as a college student. I eventually used my anger as fuel however and graduated at the top of my class with honors. In fact, the student body voted me most likely to succeed. I was initially disappointed because my dreams had been derailed by a test that has since been deemed a culturally divisive assessment.

Nonetheless, Mrs. Martin, my guidance counselor, and my mother constantly reminded me that I was indeed college material. Hence, I entered the 1990 Philadelphia Public League All Star Game with a chip on my shoulder. I played great defense and threw down an acrobatic dunk in the open court. The crowd went crazy! My mother was cheering so loudly that I recognized her voice in the crowd.

A Young Khalid on the Basketball Court

Personally, I thought the game was all for naught until I met Coach McGee of Northeastern Christian Junior College (NCJC) located in Villanova, Pennsylvania. He approached me after the All Star Game; introduced himself, handed me and my mother a business card, and stated in his best coach's voice: "You are a good player...But if you want to become great, work on your grades, and earn a scholarship at a four-year program, you need to come to NCJC!" Although, I was disappointed that this was "only" a junior college opportunity, I saw it as an opportunity to grow and continue on the pathway towards success.

In the fall of 1990, I entered NCJC determined to exceed all academic expectations. Since the SAT had deemed me as not being college ready, I was determined to make a name for myself as a basketball player and academic. As fate would have it, I grew three inches in a matter of a months between graduation and my arrival at NCJC. I was now a 6'6" small forward. I became an absolute beast on the court, and was the second leading scorer and important sixth man on a team loaded with talent. Additionally, I finished the first year of junior college with a 3.7 grade point average. I was focused, motivated, and determined to be the best. My ferocity to succeed was driven by great professors that took the time to connect with me and who remained accessible if I had questions. They continually encouraged me by expressing that I had the intelligence to succeed towards infinite possibilities.

They introduced me to books such as the *Bell Curve*, by Charles A. Murray and Richard J. Herrnstein which ignited my passion to defy the odds. The Bell Curve Theory explicitly states that minorities from low socioeconomic backgrounds have the intelligence similar to that of apes and are therefore destined for failure. Also, that people with the aforementioned affliction are doomed when it comes to making an impact in America—an ever-changing society. For many students from a similar socio-economic background as myself, reading a book like the Bell Curve Theory would be a poison pill that serves to destroy their dream of breaking the cycle of poverty through literacy. However, thanks to great mentoring and support, coupled with my intrinsic drive to succeed, this was the perfect text to put my mission for success on steroids. Telling me I couldn't be successful was nothing more than fuel to disprove the theory!

There are times when I felt the world did not want me to succeed. They preferred to believe that being an urban educated, inner-city youth meant I would succumb to the survival of the fittest. Success for poor inner-city youth was recognized as an anomaly. I wanted to be that anomaly—the one who defies the data. This led to an exceptional drive in the classroom as well as on the basketball court.

By the end of my first year at NCJC I had become a focused student and received the Northeastern Christian Faculty Award, which came to me by surprise. While I was packing up my belongings at the end of the spring semester to return to Philadelphia for a summer work opportunity, Coach McGee unexpectedly visited my dorm room. He convinced me that I should be present for the upcoming NCJC Commencement ceremony. He said it would be an opportunity to visualize the joy and success of receiving an Associate's Degree. Coach McGee was emphatic that this experience would further motivate me to complete my academics and help me remain focused while on summer break. He said that I should look at my attendance at the event as a leadership moment since he was nominating me as captain of the basketball team for the upcoming 1991-92 season. I was not moved by Coach McGee's suggestion as I simply wanted to go home to start my summer, but nonetheless I attended graduation the following day as instructed.

I arrived fashionably late to the ceremony. Though I was dressed in olive colored linen, wore a beige fedora, and Italian shoes, I was still upset about having to be in attendance. As the program proceeded, graduate after graduate approached the stage to receive their diploma, shake the dean's hand, and pause for a picture. I could see the joy of success and completion on their faces and in their eyes. There were tears of joy, looks of relief, and glazed eyes of uncertainty at the prospect of facing the real world following graduation.

The program transitioned to the 1991 award recipients. Family and friends seated in the audience applauded, as each name was called and as the students stood to be recognized. Then the program transitioned to underclassmen receiving awards. By this time, my frustration was brewing, because I wanted to be at home in Philadelphia with my family and friends. Student names being called was simply noise in my ears.

The college President approached the stage to read the requirements for the recipient of the prestigious NCJC Faculty Award, which rewarded one underclassman with free tuition and board. This award was granted to a student who demonstrated superb prowess as a scholar, including positive attitude, impact on the student body as a leader, and most likely to succeed. I was focused on the preamble and joined the audience in a loud round of applause for the prospective recipient. There was a pause in the action, then the College President declared, Khalid Nabeeh Mumin as the award recipient. I was in total shock! As I approached the stairs to the stage with tears in my eyes, I recognized my family seated in the audience. I was overwhelmed with joy and was in total shock. I was trying to quantify the impact I'd had on my classmates and digest the fact that the school president had stated that the faculty had chosen me unanimously. I approached the stage, received the award (a small wooden plaque), then dropped it, because I was numb!

This was the first time that a student-athlete had received this prestigious accolade. It was an award that carried the expectation of "most likely to succeed" for the recipient. I was extremely motivated to exceed all expectations. I did not want to disappoint the faculty. I wanted to lead the student body as an ambassador for success. I wanted to fulfill my quest to demonstrate that athletes can also be recognized as academics.

Receiving the NCJC Faculty Award

In an effort to expand my knowledge I read every additional text I could get my hands on from Langston Hughes, William Shakespeare, Emily Dickinson, John Edgar Wideman and Ralph Ellison. And to get in top physical shape, I worked out every day over the summer with one of Philadelphia's most prestigious, unsung basketball legends: Rico Washington.

As Bryson Brown wrote in The Legends Series (2015):

In the 1980's in Philadelphia Rico Washington was a man amongst boys on the basketball court. At 6'7" and 225lbs, he built a reputation on the high school courts and playgrounds as one of the city's best ever. Rico was a beast in the low post and he had the uncanny ability to score on players at will who were much taller than him. His quickness and strength were too much for anyone to handle and everyone he faced would become a victim to his total domination on the basketball court.

Rico thought the ball was supposed to be in his hands whether he was scoring or rebounding. He had the ability to totally take over a game at any time with his unstoppable down low scoring or his ability to totally control the boards. The legend of Rico Washington started to grow when he, as a 6'5" eighth grader, was destroying grown men in pick-up games on the playgrounds of the West Oak Lane section of Philadelphia. By the time, he entered high school his reputation in the city was well established and he would immediately become one of the best players in the city. He would split his three-year high school career between Frankford and Ben Franklin High Schools, scoring over 1300 points and being named an All-City Player every year.

The game that cemented his legendary status was a game against the number one rated team in the country with the number one rated player in the country, Billy Thompson. Rico outplayed Thompson, lighting up Camden for 37 points and 11 rebounds.

He followed that game up after being invited to play in the Dapper Dan High School All-Star game, scoring 28 points and grabbing 15 rebounds as the crowd repeatedly chanted "Rico! Rico!" He was named the game's Most Valuable Player.

Every major college program had Rico on their radar, but there was just one problem. Rico could barely read and didn't have the grades to even graduate from high school. Rico however, never had a shortage of people who wanted to help him. And so it was decided by a support team that included his parents, his high school, and Philadelphia basketball legend Sonny Hill that the place for Rico to repair his academic status and pursue his dream would be Gloucester County College in Sewell, N.J., where coach Ron "Fang" Mitchell ran a high-powered basketball program.

It was also decided in his first year at Gloucester that he would not play basketball and would focus on academic deficiencies instead. By the end of his first year there he had earned his GED. The next two years he was totally dominant on the basketball court and was named a junior college All-American.

Rico Washington, Photo by Brady Small

He then took his game to Weber State in Ogden, Utah, where he continued to do what he had always done on a basketball court and that was dominate. In his first year at Weber State he averaged 19.8 points and 10.3 rebounds and was named to the All-Big Sky Conference. He followed that season by averaging 22 points and 10.8 rebounds a game and was named conference player of the year. Rico was never able to fulfill his dream to play in the NBA, but his dominance on the basketball court made him a basketball legend.

In 1993, Rico Washington collapsed at home after playing in a summer league basketball game. He died shortly after at a local hospital at the age of 28...

It is clear to see why I was so impressed with him. Most importantly after working out with Rico and learning valuable lessons from the elite athlete that he was, he impressed upon me the desire to lead not only with my athletic abilities but also with my brain. I wanted to serve as a role model for inner-city youth who had the potential to not only gain admission to college but also gain glory and accolades along the way. This ferocity led to a stretch of athletic success, where I was voted an *All Region* recipient, meaning I was one of the best basketball players in the northeast corridor of the United States. I became NCJC's most valuable player earned several Sam Cozen Awards, and ended up averaging 24.5 points per game. I was also, carrying a 3.8 grade point average with several colleges looking to recruit me to a four-year school on a full scholarship. I chose to attend Shippensburg University (PA) after careful research of their retention and transfer rates, which was approximately 70% with a job placement rate of 90% for students majoring in education. At the end of the season and following graduation, I was very excited to head home to my high school to prove to underclassmen that success can indeed be attained at a two-year college.

Upon my return to visit Olney High School in May 1991, the Assistant Principal, Mrs. Horter greeted me with open arms, hugged me, pulled my ear, and berated me for not inviting her to my graduation. I explained that I was so overwhelmed with finishing up and transitioning to Shippensburg University that I only had time to invite my family to the commencement exercises. Hurriedly, she rushed me over to the school's media center, so I could record a live interview outlining my college achievements.

At the time, this was the epitome of my success, and provided me with opportunities to reach inner-city youth. I was energized at the prospect of magnifying my message and still young enough to be authentic and relatable to high school students. The fact that I really understood what it meant to struggle in *the hood,* yet still achieve success got their attention. I told stories about my ninth-grade year and though I'd failed the grade once I still managed to find success. I told them about influential educators who were beacons of hope when I felt hopeless. I shared my need to persevere after I'd failed miserably on the SAT. I recounted being raised in a single-parent home and having to eat sardines, grits, and corned beef hash for dinner for weeks at a time.

More importantly, I told them of my new array of friends all destined for success even though they too had overcome tremendous odds. Yes, I let the students know there are angels everywhere along the journey, and soldiers in the field or close friends that will do battle with you against the odds. I let them know that it was indeed possible to defy stereotypes and data and that there are always those willing to collaborate with you while committing to changing the world.

Dr. Khalid Mumin

CHAPTER THREE| TOMORROW IS NOT YESTERDAY

Near the end of summer, I was anxiously awaiting the four-year college experience; the class sizes, social experiences, and competing in the elite and largest conference in NCAA Division II basketball, the Pennsylvania State Athletics Conference (PSAC).

This excitement turned to fear when on the first student activity night, the movie *Mississippi Burning* was shown in the student activity center. Not to mention that the orientation textbook recommended by the university was *The Lord of the Flies*, by William Golding. Looking at the demographics of the students in the orientation activities I thought to myself that with 90% of them being white and less than 10% of them black, I was embarking on a journey where race was paramount and survival of the fittest was the mantra. Again, as an inner-city kid, who attended predominately African American Schools grades K-12 and a school of great diversity in my first two-years at NCJC, this challenge was definitely a culture shock.

My first week of school was miserable even though there were no scheduled classes or practices. I keenly remember walking into the cafeteria on several occasions and looking around hoping to sit with a classmate who looked even just a little like me. Instead I was met with a sea of people who were the complete opposite — white. I felt uncomfortable and I could tell that my classmates were feeling uncomfortable too.

Thus, I isolated myself in the cafeteria and sunk into home sickness. To make matters worse, there were no local urban radio stations or television shows to ease the pain.

I walked across campus one evening, thinking to myself; What have I done? Why did I choose Shippensburg University? Will I have success, and when can I go home? As I walked however, an angel appeared. This angel was Ms. Diane Jefferson, the Director of Multicultural Student Affairs (MSA). She approached me and said, "Hey brother, I see you are having issues transitioning to Ship. Do you want to talk about it?" Immediately, I poured out my fears, concerns, and shared the pressure of high expectations for me as an elite student-athlete. Ms. Jefferson calmly said, "I need you to come on home to the MSA where we'll eat some soul food, listen to music, and watch Black movies if you want. I just need you to promise me two things: (1) come visit often and (2) seek some activities and leadership positions in the MSA because I can use you brother...You have a good head on your shoulders."

I did what she suggested and visited the MSA and indulged in some excellent soul food, read Ebony and Black Enterprise Magazines, and listened to the soulful rhythm and blues of Sam Cooke, Aretha Franklin, James Brown, Anita Baker, Minnie Ripperton, and Al Green. I met with peers and upper classmen who looked like me and who had similar backgrounds.

Ms. Jefferson introduced me to various pieces of African American Art posted in the MSA and discussed my potential with me. She had gained some insight from adults on campus who'd engaged in conversations with me along the way and she took the time to hear my entire story. After a few hours in the MSA, I was committed to visiting often and made a promise to Ms. Jefferson that I would pursue a leadership role after my first year at Shippensburg University.

I left the MSA energized and ready to compete. I went to basketball practice seeking dominance. I became a team captain after many hard practices and long discussions with head coach, Roger Goodling, affectionately known as "Goody." Goody told me from the beginning that I was a leader, and that he expected greatness from me on the court and in the classroom.

Coach Goody was the ultimate motivator and realist. He called in all of the student-athletes entering from junior and community colleges, and had us look around at each other—all seven of us. He told us statistics show that only three of us would graduate on time for a variety of reasons. He then asked: "Who's it gonna' be?" Then he called us each by our jersey number and when he got to mine, he hollered: "Is it gonna be you 24?" He continued down the line; "Is it gonna be you 20? Is it gonna' be you 52? Is it gonna' be you 34? Is it gonna' be you?"

Let me just say that Number 24 was determined that he was going to be successful and beat all the odds. The

Dunking with Ease

competition was in fact as challenging on the basketball court as the PSAC had advertised. I was a good athlete averaging modest double digits in scoring, and having several breakout games of 20 or more points. I received player of the week awards and most valuable player trophies for tournaments and for the team overall. I was extremely competitive athletically and watched endless game footage, while practicing and implementing moves I'd learned from the great Rico Washington. I actually played basketball with the same bravado as the greatest boxer of all time, Muhammed Ali. I played hard,

Smiling Teammates

Waiting for the Pass

motivated my teammates, did a lot of trash talking, dunked with great ferocity, and had lots of fun with the fans. I did all of this while hearing my mother's voice in the background saying, "Stay focused on the books and basketball will take care of itself."

Kiwanis Tournament Championship Trophy

Academically, there were challenges as I had limited prior knowledge of many of the topics covered in class. However, I was driven to achieve a grade point average of 2.0 or above the first year at SHIP so I would at least get the invitation to enter my fourth year. My first semester's goal was met with a 2.1, and the second semester ended with a 2.2 GPA. I had earned my way to stay on course to graduate. This is when I met English Professor, Mr. Jim Hanlon.

Mr. Hanlon taught me the secrets to literacy through linguistics and etymology. He mentored me and ignited a flame for success and ambition further inspiring me to become an English Teacher. Mr. Hanlon often met with me outside of office hours, to discuss writing styles and techniques, all the while sharing life lessons as a former soldier in World War II. Mr. Hanlon made me fall in love with learning through various texts by encouraging me to unlock the mind of the authors we were studying. He told me to live vicariously through the author which led to literary experiences through the eyes of Chaucer, Shakespeare, Hemmingway, Ellison, Wideman, O'Conner, etc. Mr. Hanlon convinced me that by understanding an author's point of view, I would have the tools to deliver effective instruction. For example, I remember the words of Flannery O'Connor: "You have to make your vison apparent by shock; to the hard of hearing you shout and for the almost blind, you draw large and startling images." To this day, I use this approach when delivering speeches, commencement addresses, motivational talks, and keynote addresses.

At the beginning of my second year at SHIP, I took on the leadership role of parliamentarian of Multicultural Affairs. I participated in a program called Building Bridges for Diversity and co-founded a group called The Men of Culture. Meanwhile, at the end of the semester, I'd earned a 3.0 GPA which fulfilled a promise I'd made to Ms. Jefferson.

My athleticism, my involvement in Multicultural Affairs and my decent GPA, put me in position to have routine leadership discussions with the President of

Shippensburg University, Dr. Anthony Ceddia. During my time as parliamentarian, Shippensburg University hosted famous visitors who presented to the student community. We were privileged to hear such guests as Arthur Ashe, Dr. Cornell West, Danny Glover, and Coretta Scott King just to name a few

Every invited speaker was special, extraordinary, dynamic, and knowledgeable. Each one told of historic accounts of racism, and spoke on diversity, success, failure, triumph, and also emphasized the value of investing in ourselves now in order to influence future generations. Because I was parliamentarian at the time, two of these illustrious guests granted me personal access, which provided me memories that have lasted a lifetime.

Arthur Ashe's visit was the most powerful and historic. Born on July 10, 1943, in Richmond, Virginia, he became the first and is still the only African-American male tennis player to win the U.S. Open and Wimbledon. He is also the first African American man to be ranked as the No. 1 tennis player in the world.
In October 1992, he blessed Shippensburg University with the final speech of his career. Because he was an outlier, champion elite athlete, activist, and consummate role model, his words were powerful concerning race. Although his delivery was labored, as he was ill and fighting the AIDS virus, his words were inspiring, and resonated throughout the audience.
When Ashe learned he had contracted HIV via a blood

transfusion, he turned his efforts to raising awareness about the disease. While speaking with Mr. Ashe's advisors, we'd learned they had suggested he not go through with the speaking engagement because of his health. Mr. Ashe was adamant however about pushing forward and getting his message to the people. He worked tirelessly until finally succumbing to AIDS on February 6, 1993.

Arthur Ashe

Even as Mr. Ashe rests in peace, I am ever so grateful and continually motivated to keep his spirit of hope, perseverance, success, and action alive until the day I die. This experience of meeting him and hearing him speak propelled me forward, earning a 3.6 GPA and making the Dean's List at Shippensburg University in the Spring of 1994.

Dr. Cornell West's visit to Shippensburg University was the most fascinating as he had been commissioned to raise awareness of existing inequities facing the various races and ethnicities in America. As a student in the Shippensburg School of Education, finishing the 1994 Fall semester with a 2.7 grade point average, I was highly motivated to bring Dr. West's message to the students. There were obvious issues between the races at Shippensburg University which I had observed and documented with my work in the program *Building Bridges for Diversity*. There were instances of overt and underlying racism due to the lack of understanding between the races, especially between African American and Caucasian students. Shippensburg was the first place where many African American students gained exposure to living in a community where the majority of the students were white. Likewise, white students expressed they had never coexisted with African Americans.

In preparation for Dr. West's visit, Ms. Jefferson directed me along with my cabinet to read *Race Matters*, by Dr. West in order to gain insight and context for his scheduled discussion. The MSA Student President Keino Terrell and myself had the privilege of being chosen to meet Dr. West at Baltimore Washington International Airport (BWI) and transport him to Shippensburg University. This turned out to be an experience of a lifetime!

As Keino and I drove the 110 miles to BWI, we quizzed one another on the major points, ideas, and questions outlined in *Race Matters*. We engaged in a spirited conversation surrounding the prevalence of fractured race relations in the 90's, especially with the added attention of police brutality, racial profiling, and discrimination brought to the youth through the music of Public Enemy and NWA. As two young African American men who had experienced racism, we were eager to engage in a conversation around race with Dr. West, a notoriously educated, experienced, outspoken, intellectual giant. We wanted to hear about his experiences. We wanted answers for the fractured relations that exist within the cultural context of America. We wanted to learn from an expert in the hope of leading change using our leadership positions as a springboard for improvement within the student body.

The ride to the airport went by really quickly. I'm not sure if it was because we were speeding with great anxiety and anticipation or simply because our conversation was so fruitful in our quest for answers. When we arrived at BWI, we easily spotted Dr. Cornell West. He wore a beautifully tailored black suit, black glasses, and an afro that immediately reminded us that being black is beautiful. Dr. West had a graceful walk and a remarkably confident stance. He was clearly a brother with a grasp on what African American success should look like. Dr. West helped me define in physical form what the famous Lorraine Hansberry had described in written form regarding the power of being young, gifted, and black.

We greeted Dr. West and loaded his luggage into the car, opened the door, welcomed him into the back seat and closed the door. Keino and I stared at one another, sighed loudly, and jumped in the front seat of the car with nervous energy. Immediately, Dr. West commented on our beauty and intelligence as young black men taking the journey to success through academics. Ms. Jefferson had either prepped Dr. West for our arrival or Dr. West read us within minutes.

As we travelled through Maryland to Shippensburg, Dr. West engaged us in a deep dialogue around his book. He asked question after question and Keino and I returned with answer upon answer. Keino and I were both majoring in English, so answering scholarly questions about a book was not an issue but rather a challenge we embraced. However, this dialogue was more than scholarly, it was real talk with an authentic person, believable, Black, and proud. That was the day we discovered that Dr. Cornell West was "everyday people" as they say...I mean, we talked, talked, and talked some more.

Along the way, a rare moment of silence occurred at which time Dr. West stated with great exuberance: "you two are some fine, healthy beautiful, smart brothers, just driving to Shippensburg, Pennsylvania. I swear this has just been a straight road, and we have been journeying an eternity...Are you two hungry? I know I am...I know you Black brothers must know some soul food spots in Shippensburg." We looked surprised by Dr. West's candid question and responded, "Oh yes, we know of a place in Chambersburg, Pennsylvania." Now Chambersburg is approximately 15 miles west of Shippensburg and much to our delight, on the way back from BWI we stopped and ate at the local soul food restaurant with the great Dr. Cornell West.

The owner, who is also the chef, waitress, and cashier approached the counter and called Keino and me by name, asking us what we wanted. We ordered; then she focused her attention on Dr. West asking him what he'd like to eat. All of a sudden while she was writing his order down, she abruptly stopped, removed her bonnet, and greeted Dr. West. She said, "boys what in the hell you doing with Dr. Cornell West, and why didn't yawl call me to let me know he was coming? Got me back here looking a mess. I would have put on something nice for this moment!" We laughed, explained why Dr. West was in the area, and invited her to the symposium surrounding race which was being held at Shippensburg University. We grabbed our meals to go and headed back to the car for the remainder of the trip. We ate in the car with Dr. West who was extremely satisfied with the food---and the conversation continued.

Upon arrival at Shippensburg University, we took Dr. West to meet Ms. Jefferson at the Office of Multicultural Student Affairs (MSA). Dr. West autographed our books and wrote a statement of inspiration. We entered the MSA with more insight, knowledge, inspiration, and stories to last a lifetime.

Our classmates were surprised and impressed by how "real" Dr. West was in his conversations. He answered our questions with tremendous authenticity. He challenged us as intelligent young people to work hard in changing the narrative about race in America. Dr. West exclaimed, he was an old soldier in promoting the civil rights of the underserved, and that we had an unlimited capacity to change the world. After this brief, intimate dialogue with the members of MSA, Dr. West left and headed to Heiges Fieldhouse at Shippensburg University in preparation for the public symposium.

The fieldhouse was packed with approximately 2,000 people. The attendees included students, community members, activists—both for and against positive race relations, and the news media. The presentation lasted about an hour with Dr. West providing example upon example of the prevalence of racism in America. There were times of great applause as well as sighs of deep concern. People were amazed by Dr. West's authenticity as he did not sugar coat anything.

I loved every moment of the dialogue because we all needed a wakeup call. The symposium ignited a passion to become more than a bystander romanticizing about issues of racism and diversity. I became a committed change agent to making a difference in America by striving to change the dialogue and eliminating the fear surrounding discussions on race. I made a commitment that evening to no longer look at America as a *melting pot* where everyone is a citizen on equal footing with equal rights. Instead, I vowed not to limit myself solely to opportunities resulting from assimilation to the dominant White American culture and values. I consciously began to view America as a *salad bowl* instead, where everyone has their uniqueness and where everyone has the capacity to initiate change. Each of us has the opportunity to pursue happiness and success by engaging in preparation and hard work. More importantly, everyone's cultural identity should be valued with equal importance; thus, resulting in a newly defined America filled with diversity, inclusion, and equity.

My career at Shippensburg University ended on a high note. I'd accumulated many accolades as a scholar-athlete and I ended the 1995 Spring semester with a 3.9 GPA, graduating with a Bachelor's Degree in English. I was motivated and driven to change the world.

Two years later, I began teaching and also entered graduate school at Pennsylvania State University. I graduated with a 3.9 GPA earning a Master's Degree in Curriculum and Instruction. By this time, I had developed a keen focus on the importance of being a role model for the students I teach, while understanding wholeheartedly that education is the pathway to success.

My teaching style was filled with great energy, passion, and purpose. I told stories of success and tragedy in order to capture the student's attention and draw out teachable moments. I engaged in storytelling whenever possible to enable students to make connections with the texts they were reading. I developed my style through humanistic skills, making connections with students and families, and mastering the precepts outlined in the *Mosaic of Thought* by Ellin Keene and Susan Zimmerman. Through their work, scholars are challenged to make connections with their learning—text to text, text to self, and text to world.

Meanwhile I was setting goals towards becoming an administrator and dedicating myself to being a life-long learner. I became a Dean of Students, then Assistant Principal, Principal, Director of Secondary Education then Superintendent of Schools, all the while earning a Doctorate in Education Administration from the University of Pennsylvania while carrying a 3.69 GPA.

As clichés go, I can honestly say that like fine wine, I got better with age. Realistically however, my journey towards becoming a high-performing educator and academic was achieved with the support of extraordinary mentoring and exposure to some of the world's brightest thought partners. My sense of determination came from my childhood days growing up in Philadelphia.

I knew that due to my personal journey and success I would be able to effectively inspire children. I would teach them to leave their baggage at the door of the school and take advantage of the opportunity of a lifetime through educational access and opportunities.

Education is the pathway to success. Education has the ability to break the cycle of generational poverty. Education has the ability to create mobility in the workforce. Education is the prerequisite in order to take one's seat at the table and define success in an ever-changing society. Education is the gateway to partaking in the American Dream.

The American Dream
By Amy H. Wichita

It is the American Dream
What we all strive for and imagine
In double-wide trailers to double-wide mansions
In sprouting lakes of fake fish.
Nothing captures its essence
Unbound by time or dust or rot
The things we cherish still are lovingly patted
And brought through the centuries.

It is more than a dream now
It's a reality that the millions have made
Our heart and soul builds the heaven on earth.
A refuge for the sick,
And a shelter for the needy,
It is everything we desire.

In the cherry trucks and laughing children
To indolent teenagers with smoke circling
We see our dream and the actuality
It may not be perfect, but it is our heaven
And so disillusioned we conjure forth our hope.

In the picket fences we see our childhood
In the sky we see our adulthood
And in the middle we see our life.

Suspended, but not contained,
It is the dream that wakes within us all.

Historical Perspectives of African Americans in Education|

African American youth have been historically faced with violence, teenage pregnancy, deadbeat fathers, shortened life expectancy, 10 years to life in prison, racism, separatism, and stereotyping in the media. However, each year a small percentage of African American youth find a path through the aforementioned challenges. They find success in the educational system through the support of influential leadership, caring teachers, and mentorship while they travel through their educational journey.

Their success has been apparent despite the lack of African American teachers or administrators in America's public schools. However, evidence shows that the presence of African American educators makes a significant difference in fostering African American children's success in schools. The lack of African American educators is especially prevalent in America's urban public schools, where the greatest numbers of African American children attend school. African American educators predominantly tend to gravitate to larger urban school districts, where public schools are heavily populated with African American children.

It remains however that African Americans are not necessarily encouraged in high school or college to enter teaching as a profession, so there is a shortage of interested candidates. Also, when African Americans acquire college degrees, similar to my experience, they are more often than not, recruited into other industries. While on a trip to Atlanta I was recruited by Coca Cola, even though I had a degree in education. Furthermore, once African American educators acquire teaching positions, they migrate to urban settings, because of their familiarity with the demograhics and social constructs of urban schools. Additionally, in many urban school districts, educational conditions have been challenging, educational resources have been limited, and educator attrition rates have been extremely high. Teacher retention becomes an issue amidst difficult conditions.

The presence of African American educators in suburban school districts is at best scarce and even more rare in rural settings. Many of the resources aligned with increasing diversity in America's public schools are granted to urban schools, while suburban schools continue to suffer with little to no representation of African American educators. Diversity is inclusive; thus, the need of suburban schools to attract highly qualified African Americans is a necessity.

America's educational system was built on the foundation of encouraging all people to pursue living out the beauty of the American Dream. Included in this dream are happiness, wealth, family, and opportunity. American culture epitomizes worldly competitiveness, patriotism, economic growth, power, and perseverance. As a nation, the United States of America is a champion for many of the aforementioned traits through the seizing of opportunity, equal access, and a moral obligation to uphold the expectations of the Pledge of Allegiance. It was once a commonly held credence that it is important to encourage the universal beliefs of our country, influenced with an overriding theme of democracy.

As John Dewey implied in his work, *Democracy and Education* (1916), there is a direct correlation between democracy and education; thus, they shall coexist to form the foundations of education. From this foundation, the United States' K-12 educational system was derived, gained life, encouraged patriotism, and provided a free and appropriate education for all children.

The pursuit of the American Dream through the educational process has led to many debates regarding the "system" and its compatibility to fostering diversity. John Dewey contended that schools have the power and responsibility to seek diversity of thought, practices, and individuals to influence and impact the children the schools are responsible for preparing for an ever-changing society. Is the educational process truly a representation of democracy? Is there equal representation in schools? Does democracy exist in the educational practices of school districts? Does the foundation of the American educational system promote diversity of students, resources, staffing, etc.?

On May 17, 1954, Chief Justice Earl Warren read the majority decision of the Supreme Court in Brown v Board of Education stating: "Segregation of white and Negro children in the public schools of a state solely on the basis of race, pursuant to state laws permitting or requiring such segregation, denies to Negro children the equal protection of the laws guaranteed by the Fourteenth Amendment—even though the physical facilities and other "tangible" factors of white and Negro schools may be equal." {1954 #102} At that time, African Americans made up the largest visible minority group in the United States {Echols, 2006 #61}. The successful inclusion of diversity in schools should have been a calculated, well-planned effort that encompassed learning as an ever-changing process which is guided by behavioral and intellectual growth. People who originate in social environments that encourage learning are more likely to develop into successful, developmentally innate lifelong learners {Dewey, 1916 #83}. When behaviors directed towards increasing diversity are modeled, learned, and accepted as the expectation for success in the home, there are greater chances of retention of learning and modeling of the behaviors. The learner continues to develop and continually challenges the learning process, thus leading to the need for expert instruction to satisfy the learner's insatiable need to master skills which leads to developmental success. The developmental success of children is a cyclical process that is driven by experiences of success and failure, curiosity and thought, and the mastery of things learned through the influence of leaders {Dewey, 1916 #83}. These methods were a process, a system, and seemingly a recipe for successful human development resulting in educated, well-informed people.

As recognized in Brown versus the Board of Education (1954), diversity and equal access to the educational system are phenomenal issues. The opportunity for all American citizens to become educated citizens has been deemed credible and a best practice that should be implemented in all schools—suburban, urban, and rural. Thus, it is important for all students in the educational system to have exposure to the benefits of diversity through best educational practices as well as representation of diversity in the classroom setting. Diversity in the classroom is as important for African American children as it is for white children in America's schools. Powerful messages regarding the progress the American culture can make through the representation of African American teachers and administrators in suburban schools is a dire need in our pursuit of best practices.

African Americans in Context|

Even though the public educational system is well intentioned, there are barriers that became evident in terms of reaching the needs of African American students. Many African American students lacked *lessons* learned in the home that garnered them the respect and trust of the educational system. This phenomenon of lack of trust was ingrained in African

Americans as early as the elementary years, thus creating a perception and lifestyle encouraging African American children to stray away from the educational system as a vehicle for success {Kunjufu, 1991 #26}. Therefore, some students entered school ill-prepared and with inferior skills.

African Americans did not share the dominant American culture and family background that promoted school-based learning in the home as a vehicle for success. After all, it was once illegal to teach an African American to read. It could be terrifying to be educated and a matter of life and death. Shunning education was a form of self-protection for a century or so. This led to inequitable access to opportunities of learning and/or development that created a process of failure or lack of learning, including the "dummying down" of skills and the lack of expert teaching and persistent motivation to nurture skills because of the tremendous challenge to promote positive development.

Therefore, the African American student was misidentified as disadvantaged when entering the educational process. They lacked the prerequisite skills to fit into the aforementioned system or foundation of education, which ultimately led them through a journey of developmental and educational inequality which widened the achievement gap between the successful and the at-risk. This should not have been the case when attempting to educate all students and equipping them with the skills to become responsible citizens and lifelong learners in an ever-changing world.

Student Visits with Dr. Mumin

To reaffirm the power of education in the homes of minorities, Sianjina, Cage, and Allen (1997) have suggested parents should scrutinize teacher education programs to determine how closely they emulate real life. For example, African American children should be taught by highly qualified professionals, in the same way that white children are educated. African American children who entered the educational process seemingly behind grade level should have been given the same opportunity to reach their full potential developmentally. They should work with role models of same descent in an effort to groom success that has the potential to lead students into the field of education, teaching, and administrative careers.

Obviously African American students are capable of learning in America's public schools however, it must be noted that the way African American children learn can vastly differ from the way their white counterparts do. The African American's way of perceiving the world, which in turn affects the way African American students learn in schools, is a subject of great importance. African American students need representation by way of powerful African American teachers and administrators in schools to ensure culturally responsive and representative pedagogy. Role modeling and characterization by teachers and administrators of color is critical for ensured commitment of minority students to schooling {Loehr, 1998`, October 5 #104}.

Social Barriers|

The educational system provides a unique opportunity to promote many of the good intentions outlined in America's Constitution, which centers on equity, democracy, and empowerment. The educational process is ongoing, cyclical and is ever-changing. It is a journey of continuous development and transformation {Dewey, 1916 #83}.

Celina Echols indicates that over 40% of Black boys have experienced being retained in at least one grade level through middle school. Thus, the chances that Black boys having had positive educational experiences prior to high school are minimal. This is one of the reasons that has led African Americans, especially boys, through an educational experience that does not influence them to pursue careers in education sometimes dissuading them from even completing high school {Echols, 2006 #61}.

Did the intentions of the Constitution include diversity? If so, why are African American youth failing in schools at such an alarming rate? Why is attendance among African Americans in schools steadily declining? Why is there a continual lack of African Americans in professional positions in public schools?

The intersectionality among ethnicity, class, culture, and difference are interdependent and play a significant role in the profile of a student and later in life as a potential educator. The common culture that educators share is usually exclusive to white, middle-class citizens. Students that do not share a familiarity with the culture and norms of the white middle-class may be viewed as having inferior abilities, thus limiting their chances for optimum success in the educational system {Pransky, 2002/2003 #2}.

Students are a composition of their family, self, school, and their peers. Experiences have shaped their beliefs and defined their actions towards the educational system. African American children, especially boys, lose trust in the system early on. Yearly reports indicate that

African American boys are the leading group of dropouts in America's schools.

African Americans students have not been interested in pursuing careers in education because of perceptions learned about the *system* in early childhood. These barriers, which influence the lack of minority educators in schools, began in the early stages of education for students of color. Gordon (2005) implied that in reality many decisions are made for young people long before they become aware that they even have a choice.

Students of color tend to not be encouraged to enter the teaching profession by their own families and communities {Gordon, 2005 #10}. This process of not feeling valued in the educational system, coupled with the access and achievement gaps of African Americans, has led to a cycle of under-representation of faculty of African American descent in American colleges and universities. This in turn has led to a shortage of African Americans in positions of power in all career sectors.

Foundations of Equity in Education|

Diversity was not necessarily considered in the foundational plans for American education. After all, education was built on the premise that it contributes to a system that leads to white men attaining success and wealth.

Researchers have discovered several methods which may aid in increasing minority involvement in the educational system. The strategies addressed in the literature refer to: (a) positive programmatic strategies, (b) recruitment strategies, and (c) parental involvement. Cage, Sianjina, and Allen (1996) believe we must develop quality programs to help African Americans and other students of color graduate from high school and receive the emotional, academic, and financial support necessary to have a successful college experience. Then we can recruit these individuals to the teaching profession and offer appropriate incentives to keep them in teaching and administrative careers. School districts must strive harder to be more accepting of differences, more knowledgeable, culturally responsive, and more representative of the various cultures, social classes, and ethnicities that exist in the United States.

One way to make a valid attempt at increasing the success of African American students is to provide good role models in the classrooms and in administrative positions. Secondly, school districts should secure resources to provide opportunities for mentorship of African American students all the way from elementary through high school. Then, when the students enroll in a college or university, the mentorship must continue. Prospective educators from this cadre of African Americans could then be provided opportunities to mentor and recruit those coming behind them into education professions.

The Purpose of Educators|

Educators have had the power to influence school reform each time they were among the students they educated. Educational success has been recognized as a journey over time. This journey has had a plethora of activities and learning experiences connecting grade to grade {Elmore, 2002 #1}. Teachers have had the charge of shaping the lives of young Americans positively or negatively in their daily actions. Administrators have had the opportunity to effect social change more globally by supporting African American educators and seeking opportunities to encourage more involvement in the profession through power and influence.

Ideally, all educators need to work feverishly at becoming more accepting, compassionate, and celebratory of our children's diverse backgrounds. They must be passionate about closing the transitional gap between the student's cultures as they fit into our current educational system. Furthermore, educators must be skillful enough to focus on the way students are constantly looking to establish connections and create meaning to their daily lives. Teachers need to realize that for many students of diverse backgrounds, the connections they seek in the educational system may be far out of reach.

The work of school districts should be limitless and focused on equity. When searching for resources and opportunities to better empower students from culturally diverse backgrounds, one must always keep in clear focus the fact that they must provide opportunities for the students to learn and make meaningful connections. They must endeavor to create opportunities where students of color are able to share their experiences in safe spaces; thus, making the learning experience reciprocal

Exploring a Variety of Foods and Recipes

Influential Leadership Among African American School Leaders|

American society is based on competitiveness, and social economic status ultimately dividing us into the haves and have nots as codified in The American Dream. This ideology has not promoted equity and equitable access to opportunities of wealth and success; rather it has created a form of separatism and for many of the less privileged, unfortunate citizens: failure in the process {Russell, 2005 #4}.

The practice of education must be filled with rich experiences and prior knowledge of the culture and diversity a student/participant brings to the educational process. The intersection of culture and diversity in the schools is symbolic for creating a balance, marriage, and cohesive relationship through the student's experiences to influence the educational system. School leaders should be encouraged to color boldly outside of the lines thus creating a vision for educational theory that is inclusive, diverse, challenging, and universal. Each participant in the educational system brings his or her own experiences—socially, culturally, and educationally. Therefore, there needs to be leadership, curriculum, and instruction that appreciates such diversity and provides outlets and forums for the diversity to be recognized, examined, taught, and lived.

Interacting with Students

America has been steadily becoming a society inclusive of various ethnicities; however, the issues within the African American community have remained the most visible in the media and prevalent as a phenomenon of failure. The African American student has failed to buy into the educational system at alarming rates, and the pool of potential educators has continued to decline when public school systems have not acted in attracting and retaining African American educators.

The Motivation to Jump Over the White Picket Fence|

Because of the continued support of educators from various ethnic backgrounds, I knew that I had an opportunity to break barriers. From the beginning I felt that education should be an equitable, foundational, uplifting, and positive pathway for all children. My jump over the picket fence has provided teaching and administrative leadership in various school districts that acknowledge and celebrate the diverse demographics found in the United States of America. As John Maxwell stated in *The 21 Irrefutable Laws of Leadership*, "leadership is all about influence, nothing more nothing less."

Therefore, I journeyed on a quest to teach and lead in rural, suburban, and urban school districts with one goal in mind, doing the greater good for all children. I began my education career as a teacher in 1996 at Scotland School for Veterans' Children (SSVC), located in Scotland, Pennsylvania. As communicated on the Pennsylvania Department of Veteran and Military Affairs web site (2006), "SSVC is a unique, state-funded institution offering quality residential education to the children of Pennsylvania Commonwealth veterans. Approximately 280 students in grades 3 through 12 live on its 186-acre campus, located in southern Franklin County."

The student population at SSVC was 85% African American, and there was no African American representation on the teaching staff let alone in administration. I was the first African American teacher employed at SSVC. Thus, I felt empowered and dedicated to presenting myself as a positive role model for these children. Within the first year, I persistently encouraged students to think about life after high school, and how one day in the near future they would be adults with the charge of bringing youth along the path of educational success as a parent, aunt, uncle, neighbor or possibly even as an educator.

After my one-year experience at SSVC, I moved to York, Pennsylvania and began an educational tenure at Central York Middle School (CYMS) in Central York School District (CYSD). CYSD is located to the north and east of the city of York, Pennsylvania, in south central Pennsylvania. Central York School District is approximately 88 miles east of Philadelphia and 30 miles north of Baltimore, Maryland, where there is a large constituency of qualified African American educators. However, once again, I was the first and only African American teacher in a school that had an emerging diverse population. Unlike SSVC, CYMS is located in a suburban school district.

I was inspired to teach in CYMS because the principal had a vision to diversify the staff in order to better represent an increasingly diverse student population. School Matters (2006) reported the student population of CYMS was 83.7% White, 7.6% Black, 4.7% Hispanic, 3.8% Asian/Pacific Islander, and 0.6% American Indian/Alaska Native. This experience at CYMS with the children, staff, and administration influenced me to pursue a job in administration by using my talents in a quasi-administrative capacity during my duty-free class periods.

From this point forward, I became an aspiring administrator with the ability to look at the educational system from a more global perspective. This turned out to be much more involved than delivering quality instruction within a classroom setting. It was fairly common for all of the district's stakeholders to become involved in many of the administrative decisions made by the principal and his immediate staff, which consisted of two assistant principals and one dean of students. This administrative experience was addictive for me and initiated a desire to promote and foster positive school reform.

This quasi-administrative experience prompted me to pursue the necessary credentials to obtain a Pennsylvania Principal's Certification. I saw this as another opportunity to impact the lives of young scholars and professional staff. I completed a master's degree in teaching and instruction and began administrative certification coursework at The Pennsylvania State University.

After completing five years of teaching at CYMS, I took a leap and became a middle school dean of students at Manheim Central Middle (MCMS) School in Manheim Central School District (MCSD). MCSD is a small rural school district located in northwestern Lancaster County, Pennsylvania, approximately 45 miles west of Philadelphia.

As I entered MCSD I soon perceived that accepting an administrative position in a rural school district with minimal representation of student, parent, or staff diversity involved great risks and challenges. Again, I was the "first" or at least the first African American administrator hired at MCSD, and I was one of fewer than 15 African Americans in the total school district population, to include faculty, staff, students, parents, and community stakeholders! School Matters (2004) reported the student population of MCMS as 98% White, 0.7% Black, 3.3 % Hispanic, and 1.1% American Indian/Alaska Native.

It was clear that my administrative assignment in this public particular school district was that of change agent. The superintendent of schools and the middle school principal were adamant about increasing diversity amongst the staff in their district. They wanted the students of Manheim Central to have the opportunity to get a glimpse of diversity, by seeing a leader of color at the helm. Hence, I was directed to implement new programs, add new ideas to administrative discussions, and speak to the many complexities involved in making decisions inclusive of diversity. They wanted the students to catch a glimpse of the type of diversity that can be found outside of Manheim, Pennsylvania such as that found in urban settings and school districts.

After serving two years as dean of students at Manheim Central Middle School, I accepted an assistant principalship at Klinger Middle School (KMS) in Centennial School District (CSD) in Warminster,

Pennsylvania. Once again, I was the first African American administrator in an educational setting. CSD is a suburban district located approximately 20 miles northeast of Philadelphia, which according to School Matters (2004), had a student population 87.7% White, 5.6% Black, 3.3 % Hispanic, 3.2% Asian/Pacific Islander, and 0.3% (American Indian/Alaska Native).

After serving two years as the assistant principal at Klinger Middle School, I accepted an administrative position as principal of New Hope-Solebury Middle School (NH-S MS) in New Hope-Solebury School District (NH-S). NH-S is located in beautiful Bucks County, Pennsylvania. The geographic profile of the district was metaphoric for the extreme diversity in the district—a downtown area in New Hope filled with rich history, the arts, historic restaurants, and the calmness of the Delaware River. While Solebury was plush with rolling hills, open spaces, large million-dollar estates, apple orchards, and wildlife in abundance, New Hope-Solebury was an extremely economically affluent, small, suburban school district where high academic standards were the norm, and parents and community members felt entitled to be involved in all facets of the educational process. This was typical of an education community where eclectic lifestyles, arts, and culture clash with old time conservatism. School Matters (2004) reported the student population of NH-S MS as 94% White, 1.5% Black, 3.3 % Hispanic, 1.5% Asian/Pacific Islander, and 2.5% American Indian/Alaska Native.

After serving one year as the principal of New Hope-Solebury Middle School, I was recruited by the superintendent of Centennial School District to return. His message was succinct, return to Centennial and lead the district's newly created diversity goals. Furthermore, the superintendent was adamant that I needed to hone my skills towards becoming a Superintendent of Schools. I was amazed that Superintendent David Blatt had goals and a vision for my success before I could see them for myself.

After, four years of implementing sweeping reform, staff changes, and programming, I was promoted to Director of Secondary Education in the Centennial School District. This role included supervising the secondary schools, alternative education, and serving as the superintendent's designee for expulsion and reentry conferences. This experience was the epitome of my personal experiences intersecting with the future of students; who were either seeking a second chance in acquiring a diploma through credit recovery, GED programming or traditional graduation, and students that had made mistakes and were required to serve a temporary suspension from the school district.

The Epiphany|

In essence, I was the gatekeeper to and from the pathway from schools to prison, generational poverty, and the continued road of opportunity in the school system. Thus, I reflected upon my experiences as a youth, and gave students opportunities to succeed in the school system. This included mentoring, weekly check-ins with the students and their families, and at times some tough conversations with kids and families about the importance of gaining a high school diploma. My role was one I approached with high expectations for every student. This was the toughest job I'd ever embarked upon, as there were students who had lost everything, including hope and any sort of vison in terms of how they might fit into the context of the educational system and the world as whole. Similar to my childhood, these young adolescents had no clue of their future or their potential value as a responsible citizen in this democracy.

I heard tragic stories of dysfunctional households, crime, school phobia, teen pregnancy, and depression. While changing the parameters of school district policies, I offered students choices of support, mentoring, academic remediation, and success. As a young administrator, I quickly realized that I could act as the *dream keeper* who could help revive these young students back onto the path towards success. I often thought back to some of the adults who had given up on me as a youth, who'd left me with no support or options, and who hid behind school district policy to write me off as a failure. Those negative experiences motivated me to never become that adult who snuffs out the dreams of the young who are already struggling to overcome their circumstances. Essentially, I viewed these adults as negative people trying to kick a young person when they're down in order to uphold the standards of institutionalized racist school district policies without any interest in providing an alternate pathway to success. These are called power plays, where an administrator sits as king and casts students out to immediate extinction with no more than a sideways glance.

This approach is short sighted, and though expulsion may provide immediate relief to the school system, it does not take into account how that same young person might affect society as an adult—be it negative or positive. Many times, this approach sets children up for a future of poverty, welfare, and prison. Using achievement data from standardized assessments several studies reveal that the pipeline from schools to prison begins in the 3rd grade. However, young adolescents like myself, have been given the ability to bypass the schools to prison pipeline thanks to great mentorship, support, access, and high expectations.

The next step in my journey was to become a Superintendent of Schools so I could impact school reform, achievement, equity, and access, through policy decisions. After a year at Centennial School District as the Director of Secondary Education, I was appointed as the Superintendent of Caroline County Public Schools (MD). Caroline County Public Schools (CCPS) is a rural school district located on Maryland's Eastern Shore. The county is situated midway between Maryland's northern and southern borders and shares its eastern border with Delaware. The county seat, Denton, is 70 miles from

Washington, D.C., and 62 miles from Baltimore, Maryland.

CCPS had a student enrollment of approximately 5,500 students in Pre-Kindergarten through Grade 12 in 10 schools. Students are served by a total of 500 certified staff and 355 support staff. The average student-teacher ratio was 20-1 at the elementary schools and 16-1 in the secondary schools. The student body was comprised of 72.7% White, 19.1% African American, 6.9% Hispanic and 1% American Indian/Alaskan. Most importantly over 50% of the student population qualified for free or reduced meals.

From a strategic standpoint the focus was to maximize achievement for all children; involve all stakeholders in communication, information, and policy decisions, implement effective recruitment, retention, development and training for all staff, maintain a school climate conducive to the safety and security of students and staff, and acquire resources necessary to achieve the priorities and mission of the school system, which was to provide a clear vision and a challenging academic experience for all students through allocation of resources, policy development, and community engagement.

With over 50% of the students living in poverty, the keys to the students' future depended heavily on providing equity and access to educational opportunities and to provide the students with more than a fair chance at attaining success as an adult in an ever-changing society. The more we pushed as a school district team providing equity and access, the more students flourished. The work of the district was more systematic than simply looking at graduation rates.

The motivation to succeed from a leadership standpoint is a succinct and fundamental process of assessing where the students are in regards to accountability standards. Moving them forward comes with understanding the socioeconomic barriers faced by the students and their families. In the process, it is important to engage relevant stakeholders regarding outcomes for graduates, providing equity and access in educational opportunities, and most importantly, maintaining high expectations for all students regardless of their fears or socioeconomic status. These precepts and practices built a synergy for success at CCPS. Instilling a sense of belonging, pride, and success within the schools between the community and the student body was a change in past practice but a sustainable one in CCPS's history. The small student body on the Eastern Shore of Maryland was making an impact at the State level and being recognized as a model to foster success in poor rural communities.

To review data points of success at CCPS, please refer to Appendix A.

After three years as the Superintendent of Schools at the helm of CCPS, I moved closer to home to take on an even greater challenge: that of serving at Reading School District in Pennsylvania. Reading School District is approximately 45 miles west of Philadelphia, Pennsylvania and is the 4th largest urban setting in the Commonwealth. Reading School District has 19 schools (13 elementary schools, 4 middle schools, 1 intermediate high school, 1 comprehensive high school with three sites for alternative education, career and technical education, and credit recovery center with a daily membership of approximately 17,500 students (80.7% Latino, 9.3% Black, 6.9% White, 2.5% Multiracial, 0.5 % Asian, 93% Economically Disadvantaged, 18.2% English Language Learners, and 16.1% of the students receive Special Education Services) with 1500 certified staff and 500 support staff members.

Reading School District had many challenges as it had been labeled as a failing school district—academically and fiscally. It had failed to reach agreements with its eight bargaining units for an extended period of time ranging from 5-7 years, had lackluster community engagement, a lack of school pride, several pending lawsuits regarding the lack of education and achievement for Special Education and English Language Learners, and a constant changing of Superintendents. Before my arrival, they'd had four Superintendents in five years.

Spending Time with Students

From a strategic standpoint or "systems approach," the process to attain success in Reading School District began with leading efforts in implementing a five-year strategic plan focusing on; creating safe schools, increasing academic achievement, demanding equity and access in every facet of the educational process, communications/engagement to inform, energize, and mobilize stakeholders, and financial and operational effectiveness to ensure that decisions were being made in fiduciarily responsible ways.

In unison with the strategic plan for the district, I along with my dynamic leadership team, led the effort to launch a five-year fiscal sustainability plan. The five-year plan was eventually used as a model to help school districts in Pennsylvania avoid being taken over by the

Pennsylvania Department of Education oversight and control.

Our strategy was to audit the finances, project revenues and expenditures with great accuracy, and manage the school district debt with great agility. We constantly analyzed the financial landscape and financial markets in regards to financing and refinancing debt without compromising resources at the classroom level. Even though the financial sustainability plan was an immense task with many challenges, as the leader I eventually encouraged my team to take this process and message it statewide, as it had proven to be successful by bringing a financially unstable school district back to life.

The strategic and fiscal sustainability plans were not simply procedural exercises addressing what needed to be done in theory and in practice; but rather a snapshot of the purpose of education and a reminder that it is one of the major pillars of social justice in America. Thus, bearing the responsibility of educating thousands of kids in poverty, my team and I took our message on the road — statewide and on a national level.

The hard work paid off, and our model served to initiate the historic passing of a bipartisan, bicameral Pennsylvania Basic Education Funding Commission (BEFC) formula for schools in Pennsylvania. It primarily addresses students living in poverty, students who receive special education, and English Language Learning programming. It also prompted a brief moratorium on standardized tests that do not address the whole child as a learner.

Historic Passing of a Bipartisan, Bicameral Pennsylvania (BEFC) Formula for Schools in Pennsylvania

As communicated in the Primer, by the Pennsylvania House Democrat Appropriations Committee Chairman, Joe Markosek (2018), the BEFC formula is student-based, meaning a district's share of state funding is tied to its share of the student population. However, each school district is not given the same amount of state funding per student which is unfair and ignores the vast differences in local resources available to districts. It also ignores well research-supported evidence that some students require more resources than others to succeed.

As visualized in Figure 1, after starting with an accurate student count, the BEFC formula applies a series of weights to categories of students. The added weights for certain groups of students is recognition of a higher cost to educate that group. The resulting weighted student count is then adjusted based on district factors to arrive at a weighted and adjusted student count. Finally, a district's share of funding under the BEFC formula is simply its share of the statewide weighted and adjusted student count.

In other words, under the BEFC formula, each district receives the same amount of state funding per weighted and adjusted student count.

Figure 1

Weighted Basic Education Student Headcount Equation

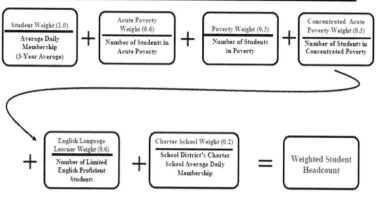

Funding Distribution Number Equation

Final School District Distribution Equation

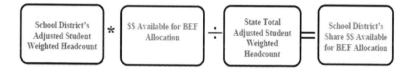

89

Furthermore, Pennsylvania Auditor General Eugene DePasquale conducted financial audits in 2013 that communicate gloomy findings for the Reading School District. However, in August 2018, Auditor General DePasquale visited the Reading School District with findings from a follow up audit and declared that the district's turnaround is one that was unparalleled and unprecedented.

Auditor General Eugene DePasquale

"When I last checked in on Reading School District, it was on the verge of a state takeover because of how poorly managed the district was," DePasquale said. "It is now a prime example of the major positive changes that can occur when school officials take our recommendations seriously and the community support is there to help. Thanks to help from the Berks County Intermediate Unit, the district hired two outstanding financial administrators who have private-sector experience," DePasquale said. "Later in 2014, the district hired Dr. Khalid Mumin as superintendent. With these capable leaders at the helm for the last four years, dramatic improvements have taken place in how the district is run," DePasquale said.

The keys to our collective success began with a fundamental vision rooted in understanding the demographics of the community and in appreciating the gifts of a diverse population of students. It was vital to us to give voice to the stakeholders; students, parents, staff, business partners, and higher institutions of learning. We recognized poverty as a challenge for students but not a death sentence.

These profound and fundamental efforts allowed us to mobilize a community of learners around the importance of promoting social justice. We were determined to ensure that a student's zip code would not equate to limited access to a quality education.

In many instances the nexus of poverty as relates to low academic achievement begins with low expectations for

91

student learning. Often a shared consensus exists that students will never make it out of the generational process of poverty. Our greatest challenge was in changing the mindset and tendency to use poverty as an excuse for failure. We were determined to reframe it as a badge of honor earned when a student competes to the fullest extent in school, community, and the workplace.

Early in my tenure as superintendent, an emergency situation occurred when a massive student fight involving four students, but with roughly five hundred bystanders, including students and adults. Immediately, the building administration went in to crisis response mode, as my assistant superintendent and I headed towards the fracas. When we arrived what we saw was mind-boggling. Both the students and the adults were out of control and attempting to keep law enforcement and school district personnel from stopping the fight. Once we eventually intervened and managed to calm things down, or so we thought; subsequent disruptions began when the adults started facing off against law enforcement. Again, another unbelievable sight. The behavior of the adults was as disappointing as that of the students.

I immediately engaged in discussions with student bystanders in an attempt to understand the source of their anger towards the peacemakers, law enforcement, and administrators who had attempted to stop the fight. What I found was a cadre of youth who felt hopeless, disenfranchised, disengaged, and disconnected from the school and community. I also discovered their level of anger and frustration at living in poverty. The kids really felt this was how they had to behave in order to gain "respect" and to keep from being disrespected in their neighborhood. One young lady said to me: "Look mister superintendent, you don't understand... My cousin was in the fight and she is from the Northside, so I gotta' rep my hood...I don't care if I get locked up for fighting for my hood...You don't understand!" Then she took off running down the street.

Instead of looking at this situation as a total disgrace, I listened to what she said and began to plan how we might bounce back with ferocity. What could we do to instill hope in the students and expect better behavior from everyone involved? I used the media to communicate my disappointment in the way they'd conducted themselves and to make a case for setting higher expectations for both the students and the adults. I simply stated, "this behavior will not be tolerated, and we have to do better as a community." The adults must be the role models in academic and behavioral reform in order to help provide the students with a clear view of the increased expectations and the good that can come from success.

This led to the formation of a leadership squad at the high school level designed to gauge student voice.

The leadership squad consisted of 30 students from the high school from various backgrounds who met with me to provide information regarding issues and solutions for student success. Second, two community forums were held with the adults to discuss behavioral expectations for them as well as for the children, because after all, schools should be safe havens and institutions of learning. We demanded a decorum of respect for the process of education, discourse with professionals and unison for having high expectation for student success.

Chad Dion Lassiter, Executive Director,
PA Human Relations Commission

Our efforts lead to an unsurpassed form of leadership which helped change everyone's mindset towards mobilizing youth and communities out of poverty.

These pivotal steps led to an effective partnership between the Reading School District and a privately owned business. This business partner was the great Albert Boscov, President and CEO of the famous Boscov's department store chain, and the leader of the initiative was Mr. Craig Poole, the General Manger for the Boscov owned Doubletree by Hilton in Reading. Mr. Boscov was a true visionary. Early in my tenure as superintendent he invited me to a meeting with himself and Craig Poole to discuss my plans to lead the Reading School District. The meeting was sometimes interrupted as employees proudly stopped in to say hello, share stories about vacationing, and even to introduce newborns.

That day, I clearly remember Mr. Boscov revealing a blueprint of the new Doubletree he planned to build. He asked me to tell him what I saw on the drawings. I told him it looked like an extraordinary hotel with five-star amenities unparalleled to any Doubletree Hilton I'd ever visited. He smiled and told me that his intent was to provide the City of Reading, which at the time was recognized as one of the top 10 poorest cities in the United States, with the best Doubletree in the world.

For a more comprehensive list of data points of success at RSD, please refer to Appendix B

With Mr. Craig Poole,

With PA Governor Tom Wolf

He then asked me what my immediate needs were for the Reading School District and how much money I thought it would take to accomplish my goals. I said that I did not know the costs yet, as I was still conducting a 90-day entry plan, but I knew for certain that I needed summer employment opportunities for the students as well as job prospects for parents to obtain full-time employment.

At that very moment, Mr. Poole lit up with great confidence as he looked me in the eye and told me of his vision for the Doubletree Hilton. He said his goal was to have a majority *walk to work* staff, which would include both students and parents as previously stated. Secondly, Mr. Poole said that the Doubletree would become the entertainment and hospitality mecca for the city and the world, and that he was depending on me to provide skilled graduates with the potential of fulltime employment.

At the Doubletree grand opening gala, I was Mr. Poole's special guest, as he revealed a staff that was in fact 72% walk to work. He had them share their stories of poverty, resilience, education, and the importance of access to the workforce. As I looked at those on the stage and listened to each of their stories, I saw my students, families, and stakeholders beaming with pride at being part of these ever-increasing efforts surrounding workforce development. We were beginning to truly understand the value and importance of the school district as a major partner in these efforts.

As a result, in December 2016, the Doubletree Hilton in Reading, received the accolade of *Best Hilton in the World*. This example resonated as the infinite possibilities education, workforce development, and partnerships play in uplifting a school district, enhancing the local economy, while establishing prowess internationally as a powerhouse in the hospitality industry.

Again, this is what high expectations for a community of learners can lead to—infinite success! Children in poverty need to have vivid relatable examples of sustainable success. We also need to provide incentives within their immediate view and grasp in order to keep them motivated to obtain academic success.

Reading, PA School Board of Directors!

Poverty-Ii –

By Palas Kumar Ray

*Satiated, desiring but not having enough food to offer
some, is also poverty,
Sheltered, wishing, but failing to accommodate a guest, is
also poverty,
Treated, prescribed, but unable to afford better
treatment is also poverty,
Clothed, requiring but can't afford sufficient to meet the
need is also poverty,
Educating, meritorious, but failing to provide better
education is also poverty,
Social, invited but avoiding a ceremony to avoid buying a
gift is also poverty,
Celebration, aspiring but fearing expenses not celebrating
is also poverty,
Friend in distress, desiring but incompetent to help a
friend is also poverty,
Oppressed, rights denied, deciding but failing to buy
Justice is also poverty,
Time elapsed but not repaying debts for not having
money is also poverty.*

Eyes on the Prize|

Reminiscing on my youth, I remember growing up in poverty and wondering if there was a realistic chance at becoming a success. I remember what overt examples of success looked like. They generally involved dreaming of playing professional basketball, making music—rhythm and blues or rap, going to college and becoming a success of some kind or opening a business in the neighborhood. There were always the quintessential neighborhood drug dealers who flashed their version of success by flaunting material possessions and lavish spending. The dealers dangled toys, luring kids into the business, because children in poverty needed to see success in order to want to become a success.

I became an exceptional basketball player, but my father taught me at an early age that exceptional players do not often make it to professional levels. However, phenomenal basketball players partake in professional opportunities and the most elite ones make it to some measure of stardom. Therefore, my parents always challenged me to compete to the best of my abilities while continually nurturing my brain. If professional basketball was my destiny, it would happen, but either way, I would need a good education to have a sustainable impact on society.

During the 1985 basketball season, I approached my father with a request for a pair of Air Jordan sneakers. I remember that at the time they cost $100. I'd prepared a compelling argument: since I was emerging as a basketball player, I needed the finest equipment to compete with the best athletes. Moreover, I had watched commercials with Spike Lee sitting atop a rim saying, "do you know, do you know, do you know?" while Michael Jordan flashed his best moves and dunked the ball. I too wanted to be "Just like Mike." I was convinced I could excel at an elite level, but I needed those shoes...

My father listened carefully to my sales pitch then began to laugh. He said, "son the sneakers are not going to make you run any faster, jump any higher or score any more points. Talk to me about how your grades are rising, how your thinking is becoming more developed, your reading becoming more advanced and about your plans following high school... Once you can answer these questions, we can then begin discussions surrounding the Michael Air Jordan sneakers and how you plan on bringing $50 to the table." I was deeply disappointed and promptly corrected my father by telling him the sneakers are called "Jordan's" not Michael Air Jordan's! I left home with a clearer understanding of Dad's position: that it's not about a player's equipment, but rather about a player's talent level. He believed that as long as I put in the work, I could become a decent ball player while mastering sound academics and knowledge at the same time.

I was a rapper for a short period of time, mostly making demos with my crew of three. In our music we spoke of community awareness, social justice, and poverty inspired by music samples of Gil Scott Heron's music. As a group, we had a great recipe, live music with drums, old school music being scratched, mixed and looped, while I controlled the microphone. Our most memorable performance was at a show at Cheyney University, where we did a live rap with Gil Scott's, *The Revolution will not be Televised* being looped and mixed over a heavy hip hop bass line, while our drummer absolutely mesmerized the audience. I was ecstatic, and we made $1,000 that evening. However, the money had to be distributed amongst the group, leaving us with roughly $300 each after paying for food and beverages. I was fifteen years old at the time, and $300 was great for two hours of work, but I knew it was not sustainable. We were average performers at best, and I was not willing to invest my energy in becoming a rap success. That was hard work with no guarantees. My father was excited about the music, since I was able to logically put words to great music of old school artists, and he was impressed that I'd already decided this was not the dream I was chasing to shape my future.

Though neighborhood drug dealers flashed wealth with brand new luxury cars, big gold chains, and stacks of money, I knew this was not an option for me either. My mother was ferocious in reminding me that the lifestyle and life span of a drug dealer was temporary and ultimately leads to time in prison or death by age 25. Besides, I already knew several acquaintances who had gone from just being regular neighborhood kids caught in the struggles of poverty, to getting tangled up in drug dealing in their teenage years.

I remember one of my childhood friends we affectionately called Muscles. He was a phenomenal basketball player who could jump higher than anyone I have ever seen to this day. Muscles used to jump over people on the basketball court during games, and he was the first athlete I had ever seen jump over a car to dunk a basketball. This was back in the 80's! Muscles could place and remove objects from the top of the backboard during his dunk routines, which was simply amazing. However, Muscles had an infinity for street life.

Competitive and gifted as he was as an athlete, he had a widely known reputation for engaging in street battles. He was known for knocking someone unconscious with one punch then taking their money, products, and wares. Muscles' life ended in 1986. He was hanging on a corner with one of my close friends from our music group. He told my friend he'd better leave when he saw a group of young men walking towards them. Muscles said they were going to kill him. As the group approached, my younger friend ran as directed. Muscles was shot approximately 10 times and later pronounced dead at the scene.

That event changed my life and to this day my friend, the one who was at the scene, has not spoken about those last moments of Muscles' life. In fact, his life took dramatic turns after that event, as he was traumatized and never fully recovered. I on the other hand, used that tragedy as motivation to stay focused on the true dream: getting out of the neighborhood by using education as a pathway to success. Today, as an educational leader, I always tell kids, "whatever your goals are in life, you must be fully committed to having 10 toes in the game. If you attempt to have five toes in the game while having five toes in the street life---the streets will win every single time!"

Educators who lead in school districts where poverty is pervasive, must have the savvy and skills to connect with the children and families they lead. The best educators are those who are able to tell stories of both adversity and success with great authenticity. Unfortunately, trauma happens at a rapid pace in urban environments. Thus, the key to connecting with students in these settings is not to sentimentalize the trauma they see as an excuse for low expectations. Rather, traumatic events must be seen as opportunities to build resilience in young people and used to foster a realistic passion for success. This is equally important for both boys and girls living in poverty. While crime, jail time, and death are major traumatic experiences for boys, abuse, pregnancy, and abandonment are equally distressing for girls living in poverty.

Educating every single young person is a challenge, as you must create a vision that is attainable for all kids. The best stories to help guide children towards success are those that are authentic and part of the educators' experiences.

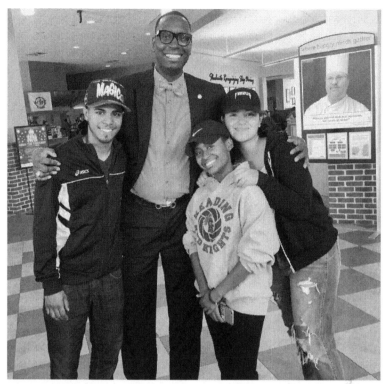

Always a Pleasure When Alumni Pay us a Visit

Stories that can be aligned with what is really happening in the students' environments. The educator has to be forever committed to being in touch with what it is like to be a student living in poverty. As the ebbs and flows of events change in urban environments, educational leaders must stay abreast of what is happening in order to maintain the keen ability to understand where students are coming from in terms of their experiences and mindset about success. While this is not a textbook approach laced in theories learned in college, it is a learned ability that helps us to form positive relationships with students. We must learn to meet them where they are, and boldly lead them towards the promised land of success.

I listen to their music, study their trends, and listen to their comments by engaging in discussions. I frequently visit neighborhood events, walk to schools, and eagerly learn from the students. I openly and continually push high expectations for the children and staff pertaining to my expectations of success. I fully communicate my belief in the education process and in its role in breaking the daunting cycle of poverty.

For example, early in my tenure at Reading School District, I received a complaint from one of my principals regarding an air handler malfunction in an elementary school. I was told that the air temperature in the classrooms was approaching 90 degrees. Accompanied by my Assistant Superintendent I immediately left the administration building and walked the three blocks on foot towards the school. As we entered the school building, we immediately felt the stifling heat and I began to sweat profusely. The lights were dimmed in the building in an attempt to keep the temperatures down, and despite the heat, the teachers were taking great care of the students and teaching at high levels. The teachers were also sweating profusely, while the students stayed focused on their studies. My assistant and I travelled to the rooftop and met with a technician assigned to examine the issues with the air handler. The technician stated, he had good news and bad news. The good news was that the handler could be repaired. The bad news was that a used replacement part would not guarantee a long-term solution and would take a few days to locate and install. While a brand-new, more expensive part could guarantee longevity and could be installed that evening.

Without hesitation I directed the technician to obtain the new part and get the air circulating in time for the next school day. My assistant and I left the building during dismissal time, and we talked with students as we walked through the neighborhood on our way back to the administration building. During our walk, we witnessed a myriad of things. We observed a local resident spray painting a car part right in the middle of the sidewalk, forcing the students to calmly walk out into the busy street to get around the part. Next, a large pit bull mastiff mix attempted to jump out of the window of a house on a side street, which startled us. Meanwhile the kids kept walking without disruption. As we journeyed on, I detected a familiar smell permeating out of one home, which I quickly recognized as "smack" or heroin being cooked or free based. Again, the kids just kept walking and playing without disruption. When we returned to the office, I asked my assistant to describe what he'd seen.

The assistant superintendent described just about everything I'd seen. Then I asked him, "what didn't you

Showcasing Student Work

see?" He paused to think, and unable to answer, I stated, "air conditioners," which led to a reflective moment. The students in the buildings were fine with the high temperatures in the classrooms because they had become acclimated to enduring high temperatures at home.

It is our responsibility as educators to work hard at setting high expectations and at creating the necessary conditions in our buildings to reflect the same. Proper air and ventilation should be a given as this can in and of itself become a motivator for students. The mere experience of access to quality educational facilities may become part of the pathway to success. It inspires some to reflect upon the stifling heat in their homes then determine to set their sights on housing with air conditioning.

We as educators have to remain ever so motivating, diligent, and willing to make connections to the students' experiences and how those experiences can lead to future success. The stifling heat may be their present situation but setting goals for the future and allowing students to build resilience, perseverance, and confidence to succeed is our responsibility. Additionally, taking a leadership journey through the neighborhood every so often allows educators to gain an understanding of the many challenges our students face. Recognizing how even the few minutes they spend walking to and from school can impact their mindset and performance.

Following Quarterly "Equity Walk"

CHAPTER SIX| THEORY AND PRACTICE
                                THROUGH THE YEARS

Education in an Ever-Changing Society|

Obtaining a quality education is paramount to living the
American Dream especially since opportunities in the
workforce have become more complex requiring more of
an aptitude for English, mathematics, and science. Even
college admission has become an ultracompetitive
process, demanding skills in math, science, technology,
and engineering.

In the late 1600's, education in America was provided
mostly for middle to upper-class white men. The
education of upper-class boys was considered a pathway
to success. It was designed to ensure intellectual
freedom, and the ability to influence the future of
education, the national economy, and the political
landscape. However, through upheaval and reform,
schools based on a particular religion, gender, race or
learning abilities began to emerge. Education began to
differ vastly by region, demographics, and settings;
urban, suburban, rural, public, parochial, private,
homeschooling, charter, and cyber schools.

As the times have changed, the demands on the
educational system have changed as well. Societal issues
such as poverty, discrimination, war—civil and abroad,

politics, policy, educational theories/movements, and school shootings have forever changed the way we educate children. There are several movements that have continually influenced educators to make quality schooling more accessible to all. Because of the ever-changing demands of a global society it is important to strive to provide rigorous pedagogical experiences. It is also necessary to remain responsive to an evolving society and to stay in touch with the times and experiences of our youth.

Professional Development:
Learning Spanish to Reach Spanish-Speaking Students

In the early years, there was a relatively clear consensus amongst adults regarding theories, class, religion, race, socioeconomic status, learning abilities, and policies in terms of how we should educate students. Eventually many theories and actions were presented with great expertise, though many were controversial and essentially used as a means to create further separation between social groups. Hence, the emergence of specialized schools of education, specialized schools of thought, and a plethora of standardized and intelligence tests made their way into the public education system. Succinctly, there were hundreds of movements and ideals that impacted public education as early as the late 1600's.

American Educational History: Timeline|

Dr. Edmund Sass, Professor Emeritus of the Education, College of Saint Benedict Saint John's University has created a comprehensive timeline of educational history. It provides us with greater context into the origins of education, the importance of education in society and many of the standardized procedures and assessments that influence education today. The timeline offers an excellent platform to engage, reflect, and make inferences as to the importance of educating youth in poverty in preparation for an ever-changing society.

While many programs and laws have been created to address this phenomenon, the system remains challenged in promoting equity, social justice, and academic success. The American Educational History Timeline reveals several extraordinary moments upon which educational theory and practice in the Americas was founded and which still exist today. The timeline is filled with copious details of the history of education. The following is a succinctly quoted and paraphrased summary using the expert work conducted by Dr.

Edmund Sass. The following information is a compartmentalized summary of the timeline. We need an understanding of the past in order to impact education today and in the future.

In the 1600's, educating youth was tightly aligned with religion. In 1620, the Mayflower arrived in Cape Cod, carrying the "Pilgrims" who established the Plymouth Colony. Many of the Pilgrims were Puritans who had fled religious persecution in England. Their religious views came to dominate education in the New England colonies. In 1635, the first Latin Grammar School (Boston Latin School) was established. Latin Grammar Schools were designed for the sons of those from certain social classes destined for leadership positions in the church, the state, or the courts.

At the time, schooling was not yet institutionalized. The responsibility of educating youth was primarily the responsibility of the parents, as supported by legislation. In 1642, the Massachusetts Bay School Law was passed. It required that parents ensure their children know the principles of religion and the capital laws of the commonwealth. Again, the premise of education was solely based on religion and law. However, in 1690, John Locke published his essay, *Concerning Human Understanding*, which conveys his belief that the human mind is a *tabula rasa* (blank slate) at birth and that knowledge is derived through experience, rather than through innate ideas as was the common belief of that time. Locke's views concerning the mind and learning greatly influenced American education. Education then shifts slightly becoming more inclusive, thus broadening the focus on more children. The mindset that education is simply for the more fortunate was challenged. Society began to believe that education is a learned behavior starting at birth in the home and not simply a birthright related to wealth and social class.

In the late 1600's the idea that solely educating young wealthy men began to also be challenged and other ideas began to develop. In 1693, John Locke's, *Some Thoughts Concerning Education* was published, describing his views on educating upper class boys to be moral, rationally-thinking, and reflective young gentlemen. His ideas regarding educating the masses were conveyed in *On Working Schools*, which was published in 1697 and which focused on the importance of developing a work ethic. The quest for more inclusive teaching was slowly but surely becoming a theme for the future of education.

In the 1700's as education theory and practice expanded upon the northeast corridor of the United States, several religious institutions created doctrines describing how schooling should proceed into the future. In 1710 Christopher Dock, a Mennonite and one of Pennsylvania's most famous educators, arrived from Germany and opened a school in Montgomery County, Pennsylvania. Dock's book, *Schul-Ordnung* (meaning school management), which was eventually published in 1770, was the first book in print about teaching in colonial America. It was the first attempt at taking grandiose ideals of education from a foundational standpoint to actual practice and pedagogy. Thus, the ideals of looking at diversifying education became of paramount importance.

Meanwhile, in 1727, The Ursuline Academy of New Orleans, a Catholic school for girls sponsored by the Sisters of the Order of Saint Ursula was founded. It is "the oldest continuously operating school for girls and the oldest Catholic school in the United States." Education providers were challenged to look at gender and recognize that from a social and developmental perspective, girls learn differently than boys.

In 1743, Benjamin Franklin forms the American Philosophical Society, which helped bring ideas of the European Enlightenment, including those of John Locke, to colonial America. Ideas and emphasis on secularism, science, and human reason clash with the religious dogma of the day. However, they greatly influence the thinking of prominent colonists including Benjamin Franklin and Thomas Jefferson. This shift towards making education more forward thinking outside of religion was becoming aggressively challenged. The inclusion of young men and women as well as separating instruction from religious ideologies became the epitome of change theory in education at that time. Education began to evolve from thriving on religious principles to examining curriculum in the core subject areas of literature, history, and geography. This shift led

Benjamin Franklin to establish the first university, The University of Pennsylvania in 1751.

Also, in the late 1700's the focus of education began to include the importance of early childhood learning and in creating tracking systems for school age children.

In 1762, Swiss-born Jean-Jacques Rousseau's book, *Emile ou L'Education,* which describes his ideas on the importance of early childhood development are in sharp contrast with the prevailing views of the time. Again, challenging the norm that education was a birthright reserved exclusively for wealthy families, particularly young men. In 1779, Thomas Jefferson proposed a two-track educational system, with different tracks for "the laboring and the learned." This was the beginning of tracking students for academia and the workforce.

In the early 1800's, the first public high school, Boston English High School, opens. This begins a trend of public schools governed by states and local municipalities. Laws were passed in Massachusetts requiring towns of more than 500 families to establish at least one public high school. Additionally, specialty schools for the deaf and blind were established for students with disabilities. Meanwhile in 1837, Horace Mann, Secretary of the newly formed Massachusetts State Board of Education became known as a visionary educator and proponent of public (or "free") schools.

This was the beginning of FAPE (Free and Appropriate Education) in America's public schools.

As more schools were being built, there was a slow and deliberate push for inclusion and equality for diverse learners. In 1837, Cheyney University in Pennsylvania opened and is the oldest institution of higher learning for African Americans. In 1854, Lincoln University was established and focused on educating African American men in the fields of the arts and sciences. These efforts were the first public and sustainable responses that included African Americans in the higher education system. Also, during this period, schools designed to educate special needs students began to arise across the United States. The terminology used to describe these students ranged from idiots to feeble-minded, while the educational settings ranged from publicly funded private day schools to privately funded long-term stay institutions.

States had local control over school districts in the United States. In 1867, the federal government created the Department of Education designed to help states establish effective school systems. This was the first attempt for the federal government to organize schools across the United States to function on the same accord. This proved to be a difficult task, as local municipalities within the states had the responsibility of funding schools through tax levy's, acquiring land through imminent domain, and delivering curriculum based on community needs. These developments provided an opportunity for parents to take more control of the education of their children. In 1897, the National Parent Teacher Association was founded by Alice McLellan Birney and Phoebe Apperson Hearst, to support local municipalities in having a voice of advocacy underneath state and federal oversight of schools.

The 1900's in public education were the most extraordinary years in history. This period is the apex of addressing religion in schools, government (state and federal) oversight, funding, educational equality, standardized testing, intelligence testing, curriculum, teaching and pedagogy. Traditional education ideals were challenged, while the Civil Rights Movement was putting necessary pressure on states and the federal government to diversify schools with equal resources. Issues such as transportation, desegregation, quality head start programs for the underserved were presented and challenged. Furthermore, as schools were grappling with these challenges, legislation and standards were being introduced and approved at a rapid pace.

In 1905, the Binet-Simon Scale, is created and accepted as an effective means of measuring intelligence for students with learning disabilities. This test was the precursor of many standardized tests of the future. Meanwhile, in 1916, John Dewey published *Democracy and Education* with its focus on schooling that produces students who can become contributors in a democratic and ever-changing society.

In 1916, The American Federation of Teachers (AFT) is founded to provide a platform of advocacy and information for teachers responsible for delivering quality instruction to students. As teachers are attempting to stay informed around the constantly revolving landscape of public education, several assessments become common practice. These assessments are used to identify students' aptitude, abilities, and intelligence. In the early 1900's the Scholastic Aptitude Test (SAT) and The Wechsler-Bellevue Intelligence Scale are developed. The SAT is developed to assess a student's readiness for post-high school opportunities, while the Wechsler-Bellevue Intelligence Scale was used to determine a student's IQ for school readiness.

Meanwhile, schools remained segregated in some parts of the country but on May 17, 1954, the U.S. Supreme Court announced its decision in the case of Brown v. Board. of Education of Topeka, ruling that "separate educational facilities are inherently unequal." It was a historic first step in the long and still unfinished journey toward equality in U.S. education.

In 1956, *Bloom's Taxonomy* was created which divided the cognitive domain into six levels: knowledge, comprehension, application, analysis, synthesis, and evaluation. Bloom's Taxonomy became the instructional foundation for teachers in an attempt to meet the diverse needs of students.

In spite of the 1954 Brown vs the Board of Education, segregation persisted in school districts. Therefore, in 1957, federal troops enforced integration in Little Rock, Arkansas as the Little Rock 9 enrolled at Central High School. By 1964, The Civil Rights Act became law, prohibiting discrimination based on race, color, sex, religion or national origin.

The Elementary and Secondary Education Act (ESEA) in 1965 is passed, as part of President Lyndon Johnson's *War on Poverty*. ESEA provided federal funds to help low-income students, which resulted in the initiation of educational programs such as Title I and bilingual education.

Programs such as, Project Head Start, a preschool education program for children from low-income families, began as an eight-week summer program. The Equality of Educational Opportunity Study concluded that African American children benefit from attending integrated schools, which sets the stage for school busing as a strategy in achieving desegregation.

As tremendous momentum was being gained with the aforementioned, on April 4, 1968, Nobel Prize winner and leader of the American Civil Rights Movement, Dr. Martin Luther King Jr. is assassinated in Memphis, Tennessee. His life and legacy become the focal point for equality of race in schools, including equal representation, quality resources, funding, and programming.

The 2000's is a period defined by standards-based education, school reform initiatives, and polarizing legislation. This movement was initiated at the federal government level in an attempt to create a country associated with high academic success. On January 8, 2002, the controversial No Child Left Behind Act (NCLB) was approved by Congress and signed into law by President George W. Bush. The law, which reauthorizes the ESEA of 1965 and replaces the Bilingual Education Act of 1968, mandates high-stakes student testing, holds schools accountable for student achievement levels, and provides penalties for schools that do not make adequate yearly progress toward meeting the goals of NCLB.

In 2004, The Individuals with Disabilities Improvement Act (IDEA 2004), reauthorized and modified IDEA. Changes, which took effect on July 1, 2005, included modifications in the IEP process and procedural safeguards. This meant increased authority for school personnel in special education placement decisions, and alignment of IDEA with the No Child Left Behind Act. The 2004 reauthorization also required school districts to use the Response to Intervention (RTI) approach as a means for the early identification of students at risk for specific learning disabilities. RTI provides a three-tiered model for screening, monitoring, and providing increasing degrees of intervention using research-based instruction with the overarching goal of reducing the need for special education services.

On May 15, 2014, The Civil Rights Project report: *Brown at 60: Great Progress, a Long Retreat, and an Uncertain Future*, is published. It showed what many teachers already knew; a decline in non-Hispanic Caucasian students, a large increase in Latino students, and the growth of segregation, both by race and poverty, particularly among Latinos in central cities and suburbs of the largest metropolitan areas.

On December 9, 2015, the U.S. Senate voted 85-12 to approve the Every Student Succeeds Act, and President Obama signed it into law on December 10. This latest version of the Elementary and Secondary Education Act (ESEA) replaced No Child Left Behind and allows for more state control in judging school quality.

The Reality of Educating Youth Away from Poverty|

As a youth growing up in Philadelphia in the 80's, my education was impacted by many of these movements. However, I did not recognize this until I became an educator and reflected upon my experiences. I must say these epiphanies were startling eye openers for me, which have motivated me as an educator to never give up on a student. I determined to educate youth keeping the realities of poverty in mind, and equity and social justice as focal points.

In the Commonwealth of Pennsylvania, the Professional [educator] Certificate clearly states: this certificate entitles [the named educator] to practice the *art of teaching* and render professional service in the endorsement areas hereon in the schools of the Commonwealth of Pennsylvania. Also, listed on the certificate are the college or university where the educator was trained and a list of areas of certification. Many of the endorsement areas carry an initial certification of five years, and with advanced training the certificates are extended for 99 years. For example, upon graduating from undergraduate studies, I was certified to teach English grades 7-12 for five years with a Level I Certificate. During those years, I acquired additional training by earning a Master's Degree in Teaching, Curriculum, and Instruction which qualified me to have my certificate recognized as a Level II Certificate, which carries an expiration date of 99 years from the date of attainment. As my teaching and educational journey continued, I pursued an administrative certificate, Doctor of Education, and Superintendent Letter of Eligibility. These subsequent endorsements require ongoing professional development to remain active.

As a decorated professional with several certification areas of endorsement, I am humbled. However, I am realistic in ascertaining and understanding that these are endorsements in theory and not necessarily endorsements of practice or practitioner-based work.

Getting Creative with Technology

I have witnessed educators with high expectations and intrinsic motivation lead youth through schooling with audacious goals, passion, and purpose and those who have the unique ability to map theory onto practice.

An educator can attend the most prestigious universities or colleges in the world to become an educator, but what separates the extraordinary educators from the average ones is the educators' ability to not only merge theory and practice in the classroom but also their ability to authentically connect with their students. This requires an additional asset—the ability to understand theory as a life-long learner, deliver quality instruction and leadership, and use personal experiences to enhance their practice and to connect with the students and staff with authenticity. "Book smarts" is not the simple antidote for educating, teaching, and leading. The art of education is a complex craft. Day in and day out, the extraordinary educator is continually improving their craft using theory as axioms but relying on authentic connections to drive home the importance of education. They strive to drive home the fact that academic success is the precursor to global success in the workforce, in higher education, and society.

It is appropriate to recognize that education has always been at the forefront of the American Dream. As Dr. Martin Luther King Jr. professed, educational attainment speaks to the core of democracy in the United States. Beginning as a tool for privileged men then becoming more inclusive of women and underserved citizens from various ethnicities, education has become a lightning rod, fueling politics, policies, mandates, and extensive accountability measures.

Though in the early years, educational attainment was designed for the wealthy or privileged, as the years passed and the call of duty led men into the battlefields and more women into the classrooms and workforce, the direction of education began to shift in an attempt to become more inclusive. There remains a definitive nexus of academic success and access to opportunities of scholarship and wealth.

To date, the purpose of a highly qualified education was to prepare citizens for an ever-changing society yet remains an ideal that many can see but have limited opportunities to touch. This includes women and men living in poverty, minorities and immigrants pursuing the American Dream of freedom and the pursuit of happiness.

There have been many factors used to separate the "haves from the have nots," including; intelligence testing, which is historically culturally biased, sporadic and inconsistent funding for schools determined by demographics, and tax base and zip codes. The results are tremendous achievement and opportunity gaps between ethnicity, gender, and educational settings—urban, suburban, and rural.

This has led to an outcry from children, parents, communities and political officials demanding quality and fairly funded education to close the gaps of educational accountability, equity, and access. Providing students with a quality education has become a focal point, as the future of America depends on having a highly skilled educational system and workforce.

School leaders have the unique challenge of compartmentalizing the issues at hand, understanding the past, yet moving with a sense of urgency to prepare children for the future. Today, this journey to educational excellence must begin with the students, parents, and the local communities served. Though this may seem to be an unconventional way of addressing the challenges in providing a quality education, it helps to remember that historically, education has always been a local, intimate phenomenon. The fact that experiences addressing small groups as a microcosm in the hopes of impacting the whole (our democracy) remains relevant in addressing the inconsistencies of equity and access.

Though many movements have played a significant role in creating unrest and reform that positively impact how we educate our youth, we still need to look specifically at the needs of each child in each community in our efforts to prepare American students for the future. The strides made in education towards equality, are not the end all be all. The premonition and success of this movement will begin and end with the students demanding to be served in schools with an equal playing field influenced by equity, where each student is unique and served based on their individual needs.

America has evolved from being a melting pot, where people assimilate into the dominant culture to more of a salad bowl, where diversity is at the forefront. Appreciation for the various ethnicities is being considered to some extent in terms of making strides in educational equity. However, the future of the educational system should be more similar to creating salsa, where all the ingredients are unique, have their own flavor, but play equally distinct roles in the overall taste of the dish or masterpiece.

Still I Rise
By, Maya Angelou

You may write me down in history
With your bitter, twisted lies,
You may trod me in the very dirt
But still, like dust, I'll rise.

Does my sassiness upset you?
Why are you beset with gloom?
'Cause I walk like I've got oil wells
Pumping in my living room.

Just like moons and like suns,
With the certainty of tides,
Just like hopes springing high,
Still I'll rise.

Did you want to see me broken?
Bowed head and lowered eyes?
Shoulders falling down like teardrops,
Weakened by my soulful cries?

Does my haughtiness offend you?
Don't you take it awful hard
'Cause I laugh like I've got gold mines
Diggin' in my own backyard.

You may shoot me with your words,
You may cut me with your eyes,
You may kill me with your hatefulness,
But still, like air, I'll rise.

Does my sexiness upset you?
Does it come as a surprise
That I dance like I've got diamonds
At the meeting of my thighs?

Out of the huts of history's shame
I rise
Up from a past that's rooted in pain
I rise
I'm a black ocean, leaping and wide,
Welling and swelling I bear in the tide.

Leaving behind nights of terror and fear
I rise
Into a daybreak that's wondrously clear
I rise
Bringing the gifts that my ancestors gave, I am the
dream and the hope of the slave.

I rise
I rise
I rise.

The New America: Student Unrest in Schools|

Educating students in small one room schoolhouses or doing it on today's sprawling campuses, a teacher's job is to teach and a student's job was to be compliant, obedient, and to learn. Traditionally, with the teacher's nurturing at the elementary levels and mostly stand and deliver teaching at the secondary one, students were simply expected to learn what was taught without challenge, disciplinary issue or push back.

Fast forward to current times; teachers are expected to differentiate instruction to meet the students' needs, while continually assessing the students' progress in preparation for a plethora of standardized tests which supposedly demonstrate knowledge of mastered content. Both time periods in education have produced countless successful academics who've shaped the future of The United States. Whether through the workforce, academia, leadership, science, technology, engineering, or mathematics, education continually evolves. Teaching pedagogy will continue to adapt and students will still become successful to further the global prowess of the American educational system.

The educational system is adequate in providing the prerequisites for young learners to enter pathways of academic and workforce success. However, there have been ebbs and flows of unrest within the educational system. The system is not perfect. There have always been issues of equality, equity, and access. For example,

Brown vs. The Board of Education Topeka was a landmark case joining five legal cases in The United States regarding racial equality and the eventual abolishment of race segregation in schools. During this time period, there were student protests throughout the country, as racial segregation was an explosive topic. Racial tensions led to a violent era in America prompting the fight for civil rights and a demand for racial equality in society, in the workforce and in education. Many courageous, fearless people and prominent leaders died fighting for racial equality, while creating a mindset and taking steps to truly display that "all men are created equal."

Dr. Martin Luther King Jr., America's greatest freedom fighter pushed against racism by confronting the system regarding equity. The civil rights movement was seen as a movement of young people, descendants of slaves demanding a seat at the table to be seen and accepted as equals in America. This movement included numerous protests and marches to put America's racists on notice that the movement would not be derailed, while Dr. King delivered speeches to energize the movement to stay the course.

As a result, the protection of civil rights became a serious issue, where opportunities began to open up, and a desegregated America was on the horizon. A *new America* began to emerge with new opportunities for equality in education, government, workforce, housing, business, etc. On April 4, 1968, while the movement was flourishing and the tradition of racism and separatism were being continually challenged, Dr. King was assassinated.

Fifty-five years later, the movement for equality and justice is still alive in various ways. However, many of the new ways lack the copious organization and sustainability necessary to follow through with a consistent voice. At some junctures it lacks a palpable, forceful movement to forever change the narrative of the "haves and the have nots" in America, especially in schools. While, consistency and sustainability are growing issues, there is one distinct tool and advantage youth have in igniting change. That tool is the Internet and social media which gives them the advantage of being able to respond expeditiously to a crisis, thus promoting change.

Millennials and Generations X, Y, and Z, have mastered the art of sending pleas for change via the Internet and social media. Grassroots advertising online demands that baby boomers and decision-makers take notice and make changes. As school systems struggle for resources, equitable funding, safe facilities and transparency, students have embraced the mindset of the civil rights movement and the Little Rock Nine by seeking change on demand with the use of technology. From social media platforms, such as Facebook, Twitter and Instagram, school age children have initiated campaigns, such as #NoMore, focusing on the plea to address gun safety and the necessity to provide safe schools throughout the country. They've responded to three highly publicized, traumatic school shootings: The Columbine High School Massacre (1999), the Sandy Hook Elementary School Shooting (2012), and the Stoneman Douglass High School Shooting (2018). The youth have decided that enough is enough and are insisting that legislators no longer limit their actions to sending prayers and condolences, but rather they must act by changing outdated laws, routed in the Second Amendment.

Today's Technology Allows Students
to Quickly Highlight the Need for Social Change

With the use of technology, students have taken a stand around the United States demanding change. For the first time in a long time in our country, policy influencers, legislators, and expeditiously the media are listening to the youth and their advocacy efforts. This powerful display of organized unrest has definitely taken the nation by storm, similar to that of the civil rights movement. The challenge going forward is in remaining steadfast in demanding sustainable change and making sure school leaders prepare and form coalitions which support the students in their efforts to demand change.

Reactive Versus. Proactive Leadership|

Too many times, when change in schools becomes necessary, administrators arrive late to the table. Then, they are forced to take a reactive stance instead of a proactive one in an attempt to seek positive results. This is evident in the way equitable school funding was historically addressed. For example: the over standardization of public-school systems, removing racist practices of segregation in educational programming, and finding solutions of transparency in how schools carry out business in the public sector.

First and foremost, it is high time leaders learn from the students, the most valued stakeholders in the educational process. The process begins with listening and making listening to the students an ongoing process. The listening process begins with leaders and teachers making a commitment to learn from the students by remaining visible and accessible. Constant movement throughout the district is a must. The students must be able to identify who are in leadership roles and have the

Leading for Equity

confidence to exercise their voice in an attempt to keep administrators current in the issues the students are grappling with. This visibility is not simply about being present at social events, athletic events, academic events and the arts, but also maintaining a constant presence on social media and culturally relevant venues.

Scheduling community engagement activities specifically designed to listen to student voice is a necessity. Moreover, these events need to occur at the schools, especially with secondary age students grades 7-12. The students immediately gain confidence from these sessions and feel like valued members of the educational process and in their own community. The ground rules can be set to hear student voices in a collegial fashion. Students must come prepared to share knowledge on issues requiring administrative strategy and support. Over time, students gain confidence when they see their suggestions come to fruition with sustainable results. Teacher input is a valuable resource in connecting the students to the decision-making process. The goals must be transparent; in order for the administration to listen, respond, and agree to follow up in a timely fashion.

One of the most powerful tools I have used in creating a voice for all students and community is the creation of a district-wide platform called One Vision, All Students and #Proud. Students feel respected, valued and safe in providing input. It provides a platform whereby we learn from the students using communication tools they are most comfortable. It is a quick and easily sustainable method that helps keep students and leaders on the same accord. Not only does this keep the educational community on message, it provides an opportunity for students, parents, teachers, and administrators to celebrate the many successes being achieved in the school system.

No topic or opportunity for celebration is overlooked. The children need to be continually reminded that they are of great value in the educational process. Second, the creation of *leadership squads* at the secondary schools provide an opportunity for students to seek positions of leadership, where they are provided cabinet style meetings with the top administrators in the district. These groups are vastly different than student senates, because their outreach extends past their individual schools, as they have direct access to the Superintendent of Schools. Moreover, students seek out other students participating in the leadership squad to ensure their voices are being heard. The leadership squad has a seat at the table with the top decision makers.

The beauty of this strategy is to stay many steps ahead of a looming crisis and in changing the narrative from reactive to proactive leadership. Proactive leadership is having a sense of community, establishing trust, and acting based on the needs of the students. Thus, when challenges arise, the students already have established pathways of communication. Instead of demanding reform against the system they can more easily work in unison with school leaders to gain results. A consistent message of togetherness towards problem-solving is a powerful tool with the potential to map out the many constant shifts in education policy, practice, and procedures

Visible, Accessible, and Known to Students

.

CHAPTER EIGHT| THE ROLE OF THE
SUPERINTENDENT IN
AMERICA'S SCHOOLS

There are thousands of School Superintendents in the United States. The role of the Superintendent in America's Schools is to lead as chief executive officer of a school district. A Superintendent of Schools reports directly to a governing body, governing official(s) or legislative body. For example, the majority of school districts across the United States are led by Superintendents, who report directly to a school board of directors. A school board of directors generally consists of a group of five to twelve members and is commonly known as the school board. Those who serve on the school board are either elected or appointed for a specific term ranging from two to five years depending on the school district bylaws.

Throughout school districts in the United States, school board members are usually community members who have a vested interest in advocating for the specific needs of students and communities. Issues generally focus on increased achievement, equity, access, graduation rates, workforce development, and college readiness. Depending on State and Local governance, especially in urban and urban fringe school district settings, there are Superintendents of Schools who report directly to a legislative official, such as the Mayor, a County Executive or Chief Recovery Officer appointed by the Governor.

Sharing Strategy

As the Chief Executive Officer, superintendents are responsible for the entirety of the work within the school district, including hiring essential senior management personnel, to overseeing operations, budgets, academics, school safety, and community engagement.

Great!SCHOOLS.org is an online resource used by various stakeholders, especially parents to make sense of the complex world of educational choices for children. This organization works specifically with revealing school quality, supporting advocacy, and providing parenting information through articles, blogs, podcasts and videos.

Great!SCHOOLS.org identified seven signs of a great Superintendent as follows:

1. *A great superintendent has a clear vision for the district.* He or she works with the board of trustees to set the vision, goals, and objectives for the district, and then sees to it that the goals are achieved.

2. *A great superintendent is an instructional leader.* He or she knows that the most important job of the school district is to make sure students are learning and achieving at high levels. He or she is knowledgeable of the best practices for maximizing student achievement and is supportive of teachers in the district.

3. *A great superintendent is an effective communicator.* He or she must make a concerted effort to communicate the needs and accomplishments of the district in a variety of formats: through written reports, communication with the media, public meetings, and attendance at school events.

4. *A great superintendent is a good manager.* He or she directs the administrators to accomplish the goals of the district, monitors their progress, and evaluates their performance. ·

5. *A great superintendent is a good listener.* He or she must listen and take into account differing viewpoints of various constituencies, and then make the best decision.

6. *A great superintendent is not afraid to take risks or make a commitment.* An average superintendent might set goals that are either vague or easily achieved but a great superintendent would not be afraid to boldly set goals, such as "The majority of third graders will be able to read by the end of the school year," and then put the programs and resources in place to achieve those goals.

7. *A great superintendent is flexible.* He or she needs to be able to manage the politics of the job – to adapt to new board members, changes in state funding and changes in the school community while not sacrificing the district's vision. A great superintendent takes a collaborative rather than a confrontational approach.

In theory, the aforementioned are essential qualities of a great Superintendent, but there are more complexities when putting the qualities into practice. There is no textbook on how to become a *great* Superintendent. Leadership as a Superintendent is an "On Demand" responsibility, where the confluence the seven great qualities must be used seamlessly and effortlessly to achieve student success.

The Leadership Journey|

There are many metaphoric ways of examining leadership anywhere from comparing the educating of youth to a "marathon rather than a sprint," and "it takes a village to raise a child." Both are powerful metaphors. The marathon is symbolic of a journey that has a starting point, many competitors, and a team of supporters along the way who encourage, nourish, and coach the runner to completion, similar to that of a traditional K-12 schooling system. The village on the other hand is a symbolic, grassroots, community-based system of support where each individual contributes to the saving of every kid in the village. It is an all-hands-on-deck approach, that still allows children to dream, aspire, and succeed through the educational system. The success and graduation of each child is the ultimate success of the village, which is powerful in lifting up a community towards economic sustainability. These teams and villagers consist of an expansive list of participants; parents, guardians, teachers, support staff, administrators, community members, business partners, and various agencies along the way to reaching the goal of graduation. Every individual is of great importance in promoting responsible cadres of young academics. However, as many clichés come to mind on how to educate children, the most practical constructivist ways of doing the work as a leader is sometimes lost in education jargon, textbook theoretical stances, "fly by night" initiatives, and "silver bullet" cure all/ one size fits all platforms for educating children.

On Demand Responsibility

The Three E's|

From a practitioner's standpoint, Superintendents must communicate a sustainable vision that is succinct and easily understandable. Visionary statements for Superintendents must be absent of education colloquialisms and jargon, so it is adaptable for all aforementioned stakeholders in the school district including; public officials, workforce partners, colleges, and universities. These visionary statements would do well to be no more than three words that encourage stakeholders to reflect, focus, and react, while keeping the overarching vision in mind. The three "E's," *Empowerment, Efficiency,* and *Effectiveness* provide a succinct starting point to guide the work of every Superintendent.

Empowerment begins with providing the resources and tools necessary for educators to teach, guide and inspire children to reach their full academic, social, and emotional potential. *Efficiency* is the art of not simply leading from the top of the organization down to the classrooms but rather in allowing schools to use the resources granted and in supporting innovation, risk-taking, and individuality. The art of leading and teaching children to achieve goals connected to the school district's strategic goals requires reframing a school system to becoming a system of schools. *Effectiveness* is the task of mapping and assessing the aforementioned on prescribed data-based performance measures.
Cruise Liners|

If the work of the Superintendent cannot answer the overarching question: "Is what we are doing good for the students?" it should not hold any level of significance. The Superintendent's job is never void of politics or challenges however, the politics and challenges should never supersede the importance of focusing on student success.

Let's use the metaphor of a cruise liner; a vessel equipped with luxurious amenities, at the captain's disposal and deployment. Every tool can be used to provide an individualized experience for each guest on board. However, there is one disadvantage to being captain of a cruise liner: While out on the ocean, it is impossible to make quick turns when the need arises. The role of the Superintendent is similar, in that the responsibility to lead an organization deeply influenced by a confluence of public policy, stakeholders, politics, fiduciary responsibility, and history and likewise, one cannot always maneuver quickly in making changes. The Superintendent must be an education savant, recognizing the gifts of leading an organization in unison with a school board. And, it is important to recognize that powerful leadership requires the empowering of other leaders within the organization so we stay the course together in promoting academic success.

As *captain* of a cruise liner, the superintendent has the greatest responsibility of ensuring student success. He or she must be the heartbeat of the school district; having a clear vision for student success, committing to leading with fearlessness, all the while maintaining expert head and heart alignment.

The captain or superintendent has the responsibility of understanding the academic needs of the crew; students, parent engagement responsibilities, fiscal management priorities, educator support, and professional development needs. The captain must also remain visible during the journey both in times of success and most importantly, during times of turbulence.

Superintendents must have the keen understanding that leadership does not happen in a vacuum and that remaining isolated at the helm of the organization, without impacting the whole is an ineffective strategy. Next, the superintendent must embrace the reality that all of the school district's successes and challenges have a pathway to the superintendent's office. Captains of cruise liners are never matadors in any decision, meaning they cannot simply step aside and avoid taking responsibility. The superintendent or captain must remember that at the highest executive levels of the organization, change does not always happen right away. Thus, superintendents must remain cognizant that leadership success cannot and will not ever occur simply in the superintendent's office. The major role of the superintendent is to empower the *Speed Boats* of the organization—principals, teachers, and support staff to be equipped to stay the course, while navigating the educational success of the students with expert agility and efficiency.

Speedboat Captains|

There is a definite shortage of teachers and principals in the United States. Some of these barriers exist because of non-competitive pay, competition with other professions, rapid deterioration of respect for teachers and principals and of the teaching profession itself. It takes a special individual to become a teacher. These special beings must possess the patience, academic prowess, and the gift to make children dream that the impossible is attainable. The shortage in the teaching profession also directly impacts the development and recruitment of administrators in public schools.

As recognized in Brown versus the Board of Education (1954), diversity and equal access to the educational system are phenomenal issues. The opportunity for all Americans to become educated citizens has been deemed credible and a best practice that should be implemented in all schools—rural, suburban, and urban. Superintendents must meet this challenge head on and seek to hire the very best educators to engage in the mission of educating all children. Shortcuts and settling for any less than exceptional talent in the classroom are unacceptable, as mediocre educators will never become much needed speedboat captains.

Becoming an educator is one of the most rewarding professions in the world. The opportunity to educate, influence, and shape the minds of America's children, our future leaders from infancy through their senior year provides motivated educators with a *rush* that cannot adequately be described in words.

Students confront many challenges socially and academically as they move through the educational system. The desire to inspire children to become academics, responsible adults, and future leaders in an ever-changing society is the ultimate challenge for educators. Thus, the field of education is not for everyone, and the field of educational administration should be forbidden territory for anyone who does not share this passion.

Thus, the speedboat, a smaller vessel having the agility to make swift changes, while adapting to the changing needs of the terrain is analogous to our individual school buildings with teachers as their captains. Every tool can be used to provide an individualized experience for all passengers.

Teachers as speedboat captains possess academic agility, passion, and purpose to be ever so mindful of the constant shifts, speeds, and diversity in educating children. There is no one size fits all approach to teaching and instruction. These captains are instructional artists who understand the individual needs of each student in their care and deliver differentiated instruction to lead children towards infinite possibilities.

The captain has the ability to connect with children through their environmental upbringing, social challenges, and academic needs. With extraordinary precision and accuracy, the captain of the speedboat leads children through the learning process by making learning relevant through those connections. As communicated in the *Mosaic Book of Thought*, the most powerful connections are solidified by having students connect to their learning in at least three modes—text to self, text to text, and text to the world.

Most Rewarding Profession in the World

Recruiting and Hiring, and Retention Toolkit

Recruitment

- School districts must create effective websites that give demographic data.
- Advertise on the Internet and provide the Pennsylvania Department of Education web link to Pennsylvania's reciprocal administrative certification agreements.
- Advertise in inner-city newspapers.
- Advertise in churches, urban radio stations, fraternities, sororities and urban community events.
- Employment advertisements should mention diversity.
- Encourage quality African American teachers within the school district to pursue administrative certification.
- Seek staff recommendations.
- Recruit quality African American administrators from inner-city public schools.
- Recruit on campuses of Historically Black Colleges and Universities.
- Request African American administrators from local colleges Principal Certification Programs.
- Recruit at professional conferences, job fairs, and consortiums.
- Conduct on-site recruitment events.

Screening

- Expand traditional criteria used to hire.
- Designate a team of professionals to screen applications that reflect the school district's commitment to increasing and fostering diversity.
- Screen applications for the candidate's experiences and aptitude.
- Develop a scoring system to asses each candidate's competencies to foster diversity.

Interviewing

- Designate a team of professionals that reflect the school district's commitment to increasing and fostering diversity.
- Determine if the candidate pool is diverse according to the school district's recruitment goal.
- Determine a list of competency-based interview questions that include experiences with diversity.
- Assess all candidates using the same criteria.
- Use a scoring system to assess each interviewee's responses.

Final Selection

- Conduct thorough reference checks.
- Hire the most qualified applicant.
- Offer a competitive salary and benefits package.
- Document the process.
- Asses the process.

Retention

- Establish a comprehensive induction plan.
- Select a mentor for the candidate of choice.
- Establish a comprehensive diversity program that promotes respect and celebrates differences.
- Provide networking and professional development opportunities throughout the school year.
- Encourage advancement opportunities.
- Avoid cultural taxation.

Educating our Youth is a Collaborative Effort

The Sea-Doo|

The Sea-Doo is a small yet powerful craft, completely individualized to the needs of the passenger. These water crafts navigate rapid turns and are often equipped to move fast, go slow, turn quickly, and jump waves at the slightest turn of the throttle. Sea-Doo Captains represent children, quickly navigating in all directions at various speeds, and at different levels of difficulty. At times, the movements of a Sea-Doo can seem to lack control, and seem unpredictable, but such movements provide opportunities for an educator to adapt and lead students towards innovative success.

Children are the greatest asset in the educational system. Educators must be committed not only to teaching children to meet rigorous academic standards, but also

155

in teaching them how to grow, exercise voice, and advocate for themselves throughout the educational process. This is how young academics evolve from being young adolescents to responsible adults.

Children change over time throughout the educational process. Thus, both cruise liners and speedboats must be cognizant of those changes and have the willingness to continually adapt. This agility and fleet of foot leadership shall be employed in a continual cycle of improvement by continually assessing student needs, then create plans to meet those needs, and implement those plans with fidelity. Additionally, providing ongoing diagnostic and prescriptive evaluation become anchors for continuous success.

The days of traditional schooling must be dismantled, as the children within America's schools are continually evolving. Today's students are technologically savvy, avid multitaskers, socially intelligent, and very well accustomed to challenging authority through succinct modes of communication as evident on social media. Rather than looking at the changing dynamics of today's children as barriers or unsurmountable challenges, we must see them as golden opportunities to promote educational success in the classroom and beyond. Leading teaching and instruction are an exercise in the education process that should not be done to the students but rather with the students.

As students become more technologically savvy at the early years of social and emotional development, educators are in constant competition to keep the students' attention. It is vital to deliver instruction in differentiated modes and to remain authentic in providing examples for student learning that are relevant, engaging, and inspiring for sustainable life-long learning. This is a continual challenge for all adults who encompass the village that supports student learning and success. This challenge affects the parents, teachers, counselors, and administrators throughout the educational journey for the youth.

As a Superintendent of Schools, whose responsibility is to lead the organization, and as captain of the ship, student voice must be considered in decision-making in terms of how students (our primary stakeholders) are taught. That being said, because the superintendent directly influences the policies and procedures in a school district, access must be granted to key stakeholders and they should be provided with information to be used as a guide for sustainable success—nothing more, nothing less.

CHAPTER NINE

THE SUPERINTENDENT'S
                                LEADERSHIP SQUAD

I Have a Dream
Martin Luther King Jr. August 28, 1963

*I say to you today, my friends, even though we face the
difficulties of today and tomorrow, I still have a dream. It
is a dream deeply rooted in the American Dream.*

*I have a dream that one day this nation will rise up and
live out the true meaning of its creed: "We hold these
truths to be self-evident; that all men are created equal".*

*I have a dream that one day even the state of Mississippi,
a state sweltering with the heat of injustice, sweltering
with the heat of oppression, will be transformed into an
oasis of freedom and justice.*

*I have a dream that my four little children will one day
live in a nation where they will not be judged by the color
of their skin but by the content of their character.
I have a dream today.*

*I have a dream that one day down in Alabama with its
vicious racists, with its governor having his lips dripping
with the words of interposition and nullification one day
right there in Alabama little black boys and black girls
will be able to join hands with little white boys and little
white girls as sisters and brothers.*

I have a dream today.

I have a dream that one day every valley shall be exalted, every hill and mountain shall be made low, the rough places will be made plains, and the crooked places will be made straight, and the glory of the Lord shall be revealed, and all the flesh shall see it together.

This is our hope. This is the faith that I go back to the South with.

With this faith we will be able to hew out of the mountain of despair a stone of hope.

With this faith we will be able to transform the jangling discords of our nation into a beautiful symphony of brotherhood.

With this faith we will be able to work together, to pray together, to struggle together, to go to jail together, to stand up for freedom together, knowing that we will be free one day.

This will be the day when all of God's children will be able to sing with new meaning, "My country 'tis of thee, sweet land of liberty, of thee I sing. Land where my father died, land of pilgrims' pride, from every mountainside, let freedom ring".

And if America is to be a great nation this must become true. So let freedom ring from the prodigious hilltops of New Hampshire. Let freedom ring from the mighty mountains of New York. Let freedom ring from the heightening Alleghenies of Pennsylvania!

Let freedom ring from the snowcapped Rockies of Colorado! Let freedom ring from the curvaceous slopes of California!

But not only that; let freedom ring from the Stone

Mountain of Georgia! Let freedom ring from Lookout Mountain of Tennessee. Let freedom ring from every hill and mole hill of Mississippi. From every mountainside, let freedom ring, and when this happens,

When we let freedom ring, when we let it ring from every village and every hamlet, from every state and every city, we will be able to speed up that day when all of God's children, black men and white men, Jews and Gentiles, Protestants and Catholics, will be able to join hands and sing in the words of the old Negro spiritual, "Free at last! Free at last! Thank God almighty, we are free at last!"

As Superintendent, I make a concerted effort to stay connected to the learning experiences of the students. Constant formal and informal public appearances at student activities and in the classroom and community are essential in learning from the students. Furthermore, remaining open to feedback from the students, both good or bad is a key to understanding the intrinsic needs of children.

Superintendents are especially vulnerable to the expeditious on-demand responsiveness necessary to lead children, as these *Generation Z* children are extremely familiar with crossing all expectations of line and staff in an organization. They are a generation of experts in receiving responses at the click of a button or stroke of the thumb through social media. These children are not more advanced in exercising voice than any other movement of youth promoting change, but

161

they are equipped with advanced tools such as social media to mobilize in an instant and demand answers through a swell of youth support. This requires leaders with the skills to respond with authenticity and speed. Yes, leadership on demand is in demand in today's schools, and superintendents are no exception to this expectation.

While I was captain of a cruise liner so to speak, a group of student leaders organized and visited a school board meeting to express their displeasure with a current but outdated technology policy. The policy permitted students to have technological devices in their possession only to be used in-between classes during transition times. A strict rule was in force demanding the devices not be used during instructional time. This created barriers for the teachers and students, as the district leadership had fought hard to create wireless environments in all schools. We had invested millions of dollars into the district's infrastructure needs, purchased devices to be used on the school district wireless network, and made expansive investments in purchasing curriculum and tools compatible with those same devices. We did all this to ensure we were including platforms online to extend the learning experiences.

This confluence of issues began to lead into a cycle of disciplinary action which was never ending. As students, found ways to use the devices during class time, teachers and administrators were forced to enforce disciplinary rules for insubordination. This led to verbal reprimands, detentions, and suspensions. Simply, when students did not adhere to the rules, they were subject to being addressed through the student discipline code of conduct. As students continued to defy the rules by not satisfying the demands of the student code of conduct, the cycles of progressive discipline were in full motion.

As Superintendent, I recognized this form of punishment as a prime example of how school systems sometime get caught in monitoring the minors, where policy supersedes student voice and learning. As leaders, superintendents must not sit on the sidelines and hide behind policy. Effective superintendents listen and act appropriately to respond to the needs of all students.

Assess. Plan. Implement. Evaluate|

Assessment, planning, implementing, and evaluating (A.P.I.E.) is a process used in the medical field to address patients receiving healthcare. The uniqueness of this technique is that each patient is seen as an individual, where the patient's needs are addressed uniquely in order to seek and provide a remedy

Mindful of the Ever-Changing Needs of Students

In schools this process is also effective, as it is possible for each student, and even each cohort of students to receive individual attention to meet their needs. At the

Superintendent level, A.P.I.E. works seamlessly. Assess the issue at hand through copious notetaking and by discovering and recognizing factors that caused the issue in question. Next, organize the proper personnel to further brainstorm, by discussing the issue and making a commitment to drafting a plan to address it. Next, implement a plan with fidelity. Most importantly, strategically plan stopping points to evaluate the success or shortcomings of the prescribed plan. This allows for the school system to continually adjust to the ever-changing needs of the students. Assess, Plan, Implement, and Evaluate over and over again!

For example, with issues surrounding the outdated technology policy, I immediately called for my team to examine it for effectiveness, while taking a keen interest in the students' concerns. During our assessment, it became evident that the policy was outdated and that students were becoming trapped in a cycle of progressive discipline for insubordination. Next, the team took charge of examining the current investments and resources of the district to enhance the usage of its technological tools.

The plan consisted of creating a revised school board policy. The plan included the investment in pedagogical tools and professional development for staff on how to use technology to enhance instruction, while guiding students in their usage of the technology in alignment with the instruction delivered in the classroom setting. Implementation was put into full effect, while collecting anecdotal data of student reaction, voice, engagement, and student success on local and state assessments.

Evaluation of this process took place early and often, by gathering data in short intervals so we could continually adjust the plans as necessary. At the building level, this evaluation occurred in the mid-points of each marking period. This information was gathered in marking period intervals and used for further evaluation at the district level.

Most important for the superintendent, relevant information was gathered at the end of each school year thus, impacting future goals and sustainability. It also helped us make decisions that allowed us to remain current, child-centered, and effective.

The Leadership Squad|

To remain current in addressing student needs, the superintendent must first hire the most talented team of professionals possible. First and foremost, we must seek to hire teachers and staff who are about student success above all else. Secondly, the Superintendent must stay abreast of current trends in education through insatiable reading and professional development. A superintendent must use his or her influence to encourage, inform, and lead constituents to stay on one accord for student success.

Effective superintendents create pathways and access for students to exercise voice that further inform the practices of the Superintendent. This art form changes the dynamics from leading a school system to leading a system of schools that has the innate ability to structure learning for the immediate needs of the learners in each school setting. This is where the creation of the Leadership Squad or team of students who have direct contact with the superintendent is of paramount importance.

The Leadership Squad consists of students from the secondary level of the school system grades 7-12. These secondary school students are selected because of their social needs to establish voice as a life-long learning skill on their ability to mobilize students to get immediate results. Elementary students are important in communicating their needs; however, at the elementary levels the students tend to have more parental involvement to spread their message. Their ability to compartmentalize voice as a life-long skill is not yet as advanced from a social-emotional standpoint as it is for the older, more mature secondary students. Moreover, from a social-emotional standpoint, secondary students tend to aggressively seek voice and influence during the middle school years because they are distancing somewhat from parental oversight.

Middle school is the age group where students are dealing with a confluence of issues—social, emotional, personal, and academic. The students seek to become young adults, figure out their role in the school system, and how they might one day fit into society as a whole. Many times, this transition is a turbulent one in the educational process, where social circles change, grades change, and their outlook on the future may also be changing. It is a time where hope and goals can be reinforced with positivity that encourages growth. It's important during that time that we not stifle these students by exposing them to unresponsive, closed-minded educators, who simply believe that rigorous academic standards, pedagogy, and behavioral compliance are symbolic of success. To nurture, support, and allow students to develop a voice is a main ingredient in preparing the students for an ever-changing society.

The Leadership Squad is a selected group of students in the school system, who want to take on the responsibility of meeting with the Superintendent of Schools. They are expected to commit to relaying issues and concerns of the student body and to also convey the Superintendent's thoughts after each Leadership Squad meeting. The Squad consists of 20-30 students from grades 7-12 across all secondary buildings in the district. In each grade level, three to five students are selected to participate in the Leadership Squad based on the following criteria:

The Superintendent Shall Remain Visible and Accessible

1. Receive three teacher recommendations regarding the student's ability to lead fellow students.
2. Principal approval must be granted for prospective Leadership Squad participants.
3. Parent or guardian permission must be granted, as field trips and meeting hours may exceed the regular school day.
4. Students must be in good academic standing and passing all subjects.
5. Students shall produce three prominent issues to explore with the Superintendent of Schools—academic, social, school safety, procedures, equity, etc.
6. Students must commit to being an ambassador for their classmates.

As the students are selected at the building level, a tentative list of issues is gathered from the interview process to be scheduled and designed for planned sessions with the Superintendent. The sessions are scheduled at least once a month lasting 1.5 hours each. The first hour is designated for the students to share, and the last 30 minutes is intended for brainstorming and discovering solutions. The monthly meetings are mandatory, however additional meetings can be scheduled based on current and emergency issues that require immediate attention. These are issues which happen in the now, such as the growing debate around student protest or student issues that directly impact them due to changes in policy and procedures.

As reported by Cable News Network (CNN), "Thousands of students across the United States walked out of class Wednesday [March 14, 2018] to demand stricter gun laws in a historic show of political solidarity that was part tribute and part protest."

From Maine to California, the 17-minute walkout - one minute for each of the 17 people killed at Florida's Marjory Stoneman Douglas High School one month ago [February 14, 2018],---began around 10 a.m. in each time zone.

This was the beginning of the #EnoughMovement to convince lawmakers to change gun laws to promote safe schools in the United States of America. Students exercised protest in many forms from walking out of school, boycotting school, creating messages of solidarity physically and through social media, lobbying and travelling to the nation's capital to March on Washington. School system leaders were perplexed as to how to address secondary level students in grades 7-12. Secondary students were yearning to demonstrate support for the youth movement and a call to action was brewing. While students were organizing and planning, many school systems penalized students for non-compliance to school rules and held students and parents accountable for truancy rules in the student's unexcused absence from school. There was an obvious divide between the laws of the land, school codes, and the youth's determination to make a difference via a youth lead movement.`

By meeting with my Leadership Squad, the students presented their position on the issue and expressed the need to show solidarity with their peers nationwide. This discussion was filled with emotion and eloquent student examples of the importance of the issue and the need to act. In the brainstorming session, the students provided examples of potential solutions for the school system to provide students the space, time, and platform to share their views on the country's gun laws in solidarity with their peers.

Within one month, the student leaders met with building principals and teachers to discuss plans for each individual school. Next, the students pushed their messaging on social media and during unstructured times during the school day with advertisements to communicate the plans for March 14, 2018. Throughout the school system which serves over 17,000 students we witnessed exemplary models of support; from walking out of school for seventeen minutes, to commemorating the seventeen victims in the Douglass High School Massacre, sit-in demonstrations, public lobbying to call on local leaders to further examine the nation's gun laws and how they impact school safety, and memorializing their efforts on social media to share with the world.

The lesson here for adults in the field of education is that students must have the capacity to exercise voice, promote change, and create a synergy around sustainable change. Being afraid of student movements is as obsolete as the one-size-fits-all days of the one room schoolhouse.

It is vital to continually adapt to the constant ebbs and flows of Generation Z. The end result is staying focused on preparing students for success in an ever-changing society. As the future becomes a brave new world filled with challenges from social justice issues to preparation for college, the workforce and responsible citizenship, the superintendent's role is a powerful force in initiating support and in leading the students along their journey to adulthood.

The students are the future of this great democracy and outside of the home setting, schools have the most consistent and greatest influence in shaping the youth. Thus, we must recognize and embrace the challenge with skillful thought, planning, and implementation.

CHAPTER TEN

To a Locomotive in Winter
By Walt Whitman

Thee for my recitative!
Thee in the driving storm even as now, the snow, the
winter-day declining,
Thee in thy panoply, thy measur'd dual throbbing and
thy beat convulsive,
Thy black cylindric body, golden brass, and silvery steel,
Thy ponderous side-bars, parallel and connecting rods,
gyrating, shuttling at thy sides,
Thy metrical, now swelling pant and roar, now tapering
in the distance,
Thy great protruding head-light fix'd in front,
Thy long, pale, floating vapor-pennants, tinged with
delicate purple,
The dense and murky clouds out-belching from thy
smoke-stack,
Thy knitted frame, thy springs and valves, the
tremulous twinkle of thy wheels,
Thy train of cars behind, obedient, merrily following,
Through gale or calm, now swift, now slack, yet steadily
careening;
Type of the modern—emblem of motion and power—
pulse of the continent,
For once come serve the Muse and merge in verse, even
as here I see thee,
With storm and buffeting gusts of wind and falling
snow,

175

By day thy warning ringing bell to sound its notes, By night thy silent signal lamps to swing.
Fierce-throated beauty!
Roll through my chant with all thy lawless music, thy swinging lamps at night,
Thy madly-whistled laughter, echoing, rumbling like an earthquake, rousing all,
Law of thyself complete, thine own track firmly holding,
(No sweetness debonair of tearful harp or glib piano thine),
Thy trills of shrieks by rocks and hills return'd,
Launch'd o'er the prairies wide, across the lakes, to the free skies unpent and glad and strong.

Invoking the imagery that all students are vessels who require support, resources, and the license to dream is paramount for student success. Each vessel full of curiosity, dreams, and goals has the potential to become a locomotive roaring with confidence, success, and with aspirations of creating sustainable, transcending success.

Schools are microcosms that represent the tremendous diversity of thought that exists in our beautiful country. As poverty rates increase, political views change, unemployment rates fluctuate, necessary workforce development skills change, and issues of social justice arise, one thing remains consistent: the infinite obligation of all of America's public schools to provide all students with a free, appropriate public education. An education delivered by highly qualified teachers, who skillfully navigate the fluctuating landscape.

It's of the utmost importance to emphasize the expectation of staffing schools with great educators. Ones who are driven by passion and purpose to grow young students into academics who will become productive citizens. We must all take time to show appreciation for teachers, especially those who teach students living in poverty. Every day in the classroom is an opportunity to move students one step closer to becoming active participants in this great democracy.

Teachers have the responsibility of positively shaping the lives of young people in their daily actions. Their passion for working feverishly to adapt to the diverse learning needs of each child, building trustin+g relationships with students and families, demonstrating connectedness with the communities they serve, and delivering pedagogy that extends beyond simplistic "stand and deliver" instruction.

These great teachers are resourceful and skillful and have the ability to focus on the differing ways students constantly seek to establish connections (subject to self, subject to subject, subject to world). Great teachers create meaning, and demonstrate success, thus making the learning experiences in the classroom reciprocal.

Passion and Purpose in Leading Students Towards Success

Influential teachers in districts with a high concentration of poverty are equipped to tell stories of adversity and success with great authenticity. Issues surrounding poverty may have devastating effects in the educational attainment of students but great teachers hold the keys to connecting with students. Additionally, they do not romanticize the struggles of poverty or use them as an excuse for low expectations. These great teachers use the struggles in poverty as opportunities to build resilience in young people and help create a realistic, intrinsic passion for success. The best stories these educators communicate can be aligned with what is really happening in the students' environments.

These special teachers demonstrate a never-ending commitment to being a lifelong learner of the effects of poverty and how it impacts children. They stay abreast of what is happening "in the now" so they can maintain the keen ability to understand where the students are coming from regarding their experiences. Using this knowledge, they skillfully help students establish a mindset for success. This approach goes beyond traditional pedagogical methodology. This is the innate ability teachers have to form positive relationships with students, while meeting students where they are academically. They can then lead them towards the promised land of success; grade to grade, graduation, and beyond. Such teachers exhibit a sense of *with-it-ness* and the ability to multitask in the classroom. They seamlessly flow between classroom management, teaching and instruction, mapping contemporary lessons, all the while anticipating the struggles of each student so they can better guide them to successful outcomes. These are the teachers you may occasionally find listening to the music their students listen to, or studying their trends. They promote a growth mindset by listening to their voices, by engaging in discussions, visiting neighborhood events, engaging in walks to schools, and learning from the students. All of these combined efforts are skillfully orchestrated to push high expectations in the education process of breaking the daunting cycle of poverty.

The demands on the educational system have changed because of the effect poverty has on educating children. Teachers are the true heroes in this battle against poverty, and from my vantage point, educators have the capacity to make indelible progress in breaking the cycle of poverty one child at a time.

Becoming an educator is one of the most rewarding professions in the world. The pursuit to inspire children to become academics, responsible adults, and future leaders is the ultimate challenge for educators. Thus, the field of education is not for everyone, and the field of educational administration should be forbidden territory for many people who do not share this passion.

Administrators including Superintendents and Chief Executive Officers must inspire all stakeholders in the educational process to dream the impossible for the schools, school districts, and the students they serve. As recognized in Brown versus the Board of Education (1954), diversity and equal access to the educational system are fundamental issues. The opportunity for all American citizens to become educated citizens has been deemed credible and a best practice that should be implemented in all schools—rural, suburban, and urban.

Inspirational educators are directly responsible for leading me through the educational process. They were a great support system, as I navigated the ills of growing up in poverty in Philadelphia. The challenges I presented as a student became great opportunities for influential educators to see the best in me, while encouraging me to keep my eyes on the prize; successful, responsible citizenship, and adulthood. Many of my peers who had similar opportunities to attain success through education, succumbed instead to the cyclical ills of growing up in a community with high crime rates, drug addiction, poverty, and an underlying mindset that illegal hustling equals respect and recognition. Inspiring educators taught me one thing that still resonates with me: attaining success should never be an isolated phenomenon. Successful adults have the responsibility to lead others towards success.

Inspiring and influential educators guided me with the mantra, "each one teach one." This African American Proverb reportedly originated in the United States during slavery, at a time when the enslaved were denied an education, to include learning to read. Many if not most enslaved people were intentionally kept in a state of ignorance about anything beyond their immediate circumstances. This state of affairs was under the control of owners, law makers, and authorities. When an enslaved person was taught to read, it became his or her duty to teach someone else.

Thus, the responsibility now rests on me to provide a pathway for all children and to prepare them to enjoy the benefits of attaining the American Dream and infinite possibilities of success.

Commencement Address at my Alma Mater

SUMMARY|

The following is a list of ten commitments, I believe
educators must make to sustain balance while being an
effective instructional leader:

1. Give 100 percent of yourself 100 percent of the
   time.
2. Believe in your power and influence as an educator.
3. Meet the children where they are and push them
   towards infinite possibilities.
4. Don't major in the minors in terms of making
   mistakes. You are going to wake up the next day
   and have another crack at it.
5. Be an active participant in telling the story of your
   district and the children you serve.
6. Make the commitment to be visible in the
   community of the students you serve.
7. Match the students' excitement and curiosity about
   learning.
8. Differentiate instruction often and have fun while
   doing it.
9. Stay consistent and fair.
10. Believe. Believe. Believe!

The art of leading a school system requires a steady balance
of promoting efficiency, effectiveness, and empowerment.
This is achieved on a daily basis through the combined
efforts of students, teachers, support staff, parents, and
administrators. There is nothing better than school systems
in which children enter schools staffed with passionate

183

educators, where teaching and pedagogy are combined with technology to ignite student learning. Wherein there exists a steady schedule of activities for students during the school day coupled with after school activities that extend learning. Such environments are successful across the board.

These activities and expectations are normal occurrences that sometimes go unnoticed outside a school, but there are times when schools have the opportunity to showcase the talents of the students and staff through the three A's - Academics, Arts, and Athletics. This includes the prominence of boasting exemplary achievement results, receiving accolades for extraordinary musical performances and art showcases, and demonstrating the passion to win through teamwork in sporting activities.

As a superintendent, I have had the opportunity to bear witness to student success and have learned the power of leading from behind as students create an environment full of positivity. The lesson to school leaders, community stakeholders, public officials, entrepreneurs, and employers is that children have the capacity to promote change in society. Student voices are becoming louder and clearer, communication is becoming more instantaneous through the use of social media, and the expectations of change are becoming more prevalent

Lord Mayor of Reutlingen, Germany, Discussing Partnerships with American Sister City, Reading, PA

Reflect on the current movements in our society, and you will find there are children to protect and a need to promote the rights of children. Schools shall be supportive environments where students are challenged with high expectations to learn, and where we as adults shall walk alongside them and learn how to continually engage effectively with them.

School leadership will continue to demand that administrators be role models who are honest and who uphold the greatest integrity while remaining highly visible for students, parents, teachers, administrators and the community.

School leaders must continue to be student-centered educators who possess a vision of success for all students and who believe that building positive relationships with the children we serve is paramount to the overall success of the school system.

We must trust that empowering the youth while helping to prepare and shape them to succeed is becoming a prerequisite for success in schools. The way the children look up to their successful peers and the great support the alumni and community stakeholders display when students are empowered to lead is a wonderful feeling that needs to be sustained.

Children are the future, so let's commit to taking the risk and seize the chance to lead with efficiency, effectiveness, and empowerment to grow the leaders of a future laced with great complexities, and challenges. Let us nurture those we serve thus fulfilling and meeting the need for influential leadership.

Elementary Carnival Day

APPENDIX A|
Some Data Points of Success at CCPS

- Proficiency targets for Reading and Math were met by the district for all students including the following subgroups: American Indian or Alaska Native, Asian, Black or African American, Hispanic/Latino of any race, Two or more races, Free/Reduced Meals, Special Education, Limited English Proficiency
- 90% of students in the Two or More Races subgroup passed High School Assessment (HSA) English with 80.3% of all students passing
- 95% of students in the Hispanic/Latino of any race subgroup passed High School Assessment (HSA) Biology with 92.2% of all students passing
- 87.9% of all students in Grade 12 passed High School Assessment (HSA) Algebra/Data Analysis
- African American students who were advanced and proficient in mathematics increased in 6th grade by more than 16.5%
- African American students that were advanced and proficient in 3rd grade mathematics and 5th grade reading increased by 5%
- Implemented SAT days at the high school level with subsidized funding for students taking the examinations. 85% completion rate of students qualified to take SAT
- Implementation of "grow your own" programs to address critical teacher shortages

- 93% of high school diploma students met one or more of the following categories:
    - University System of Maryland Course Requirements
    - Career and Technology Education Program Requirements
    - Rigorous High School Program Indicators
- District survey results indicate 72.4% of 12th grade students planned to attend a 2-year/4-year college or specialized school/specialized training
- 5% decrease in dropout rate over two years
- Graduation Rate: 87.02%
- Increased attendance rates at all levels: high schools 92.7%, middle schools 94.8%, elementary schools 95%
- Led 12 parent engagement activities to communicate college and career readiness
- Adoption of American School Counselors Association frameworks for promoting college and career readiness
- Created online system for teacher evaluation system using Research for Better Teaching frameworks
- Implementation of Differentiated Instruction and Universal Design for Learning (UDL) to enhance classroom pedagogy aligned to Maryland State Approved Teacher Educator System

APPENDIX B|
Some Data Points of Success at RSD

- Developed five-year strategic plan to address safe schools, academics, communication/engagement, finance/operational effectiveness and community partnerships
- Developed comprehensive five-year financial and operations plan preventing the Pennsylvania Department of Education takeover of Reading School District before my appointment as Superintendent of Schools
- Developed hiring practices with a focus on cultural competencies to recruit, and retain culturally competent staff
- Negotiated eight bargaining unit agreements in 3 years after 5-7 years of impasse
- Developed school climate surveys to inform practice in all schools
- Developed crisis intervention plans for all students and adults
- Implemented professional development for cultural competency strategies to improve school and classroom interactions maximizing instruction, student achievement and stakeholder engagement
- Developed six-year curriculum renewal plan
- Developed three-year technology plan to address 21st Century learning challenges

- Developed educational programming to address nontraditional, "credit recovery students"
- Developed Multi-Tiered Support System
- Developed culturally responsive teaching
- Received recognition for the 4000-student comprehensive high school as a Distinguished Title I School for Achievement two consecutive years (2015 and 2016)
- Developed annual communication plan detailing routine and changed focused communication activities
- Developed a three-year feasibility plan to address overcrowding and grade configurations in schools
- Recognized as an award-winning school district by both the National School Public Relations Association (NSPRA) and Pennsylvania School Public Relations Association (PENSPRA) for communications and engagement
- Developed Superintendents Awards of Achievement for students, staff, parents, and community
- Conducted quarterly Superintendent socials communicating successes and ongoing needs for improvement
- Invited by Pennsylvania Governor Tom Wolf to engage in creating and implementing a historic basic education funding formula for the Commonwealth of Pennsylvania

- Invited by the Pennsylvania House of Appropriations to testify on behalf of the Commonwealth of Pennsylvania supporting a historic basic education formula
- 2016 Pennsylvania State Budget approved by Governor Tom Wolf with basic education funding identifying poverty, special education and English Language Learners as severely underserved populations. Reading School District is the second highest funded school system based on the aforementioned formula
- Established a partnership with Alvernia University for teachers to obtain ESL Certification
- Established a partnership with Visions Federal Credit Union to build an on-site banking facility at Reading high School including banking, job experience and yearly financial reality fairs promoting sustainable financial literacy for students, parents and staff
- Developed construction plans for four middle schools to enhance 21st century style learning opportunities
- Developed an Act 80 professional development school year calendar promoting monthly full day professional development for all staff in the areas of equity, cultural competence, teaching and learning, safety, and parent engagement

- Established a partnership with Communities in Schools Inc. to focus on school truancy prevention at the middle and high schools
- Created "Knights Closet", a clothing donation program in all schools to address students in need
- Created vaccine clinics at elementary schools
- Adopted Collins Writing Program for high school students to improve students' thinking and writing skills for college and career readiness
- Adopted "Reading Rosie" for parents to assist in promoting literacy at home and in the community
- Adopted Naviance Program to assess students' interest in college and career opportunities en route to creating graduation plans
- Established a partnership with the City of Reading (PA) to create a Reading Junior Police Academy for middle and high school students
- Established a partnership with the City of Reading (PA) to safe trick or treating for parents and community
- Established a partnership with DudeB.Nice Inc. featuring unsung heroes in schools leading to over four million views on social media and presentations on national media networks
- Established VIP Lounges for students at all schools to promote and reward academic success, and community service

BIOGRAPHY

Since 1996, Dr. Khalid N. Mumin has served in various capacities; as a teacher, dean of students, principal, and central administrator.

Dr. Mumin earned a Doctor of Education in Educational Leadership from the University of Pennsylvania, a Masters of Education in Teaching & Curriculum from Pennsylvania State University, a Bachelor of Arts in Secondary English Education from Shippensburg University, and an Associates of Arts in English from Northeastern Christian Junior College. He also graduated from the Leadership Maryland Program, as a member of the Class of 2012, and is a member of several national and local organizations.

The strength in his leadership revolves around being a student-centered educator, who has a vision of success for all students. He believes that building positive relationships through cultural competencies is paramount in promoting student success.

Dr. Mumin is a change agent committed to promoting and sustaining student achievement, equity and access to educational programming for all students, as well as creating plans that are fiscally responsible. He maintains a keen focus on fostering collaboration with stakeholders, including students, parents, teachers, administrators, community, public officials, business partners, and institutions of higher education.

Dr. Khalid N. Mumin has a documented history of success of possessing excellent leadership skills and has been recognized nationally as a "School Board Savvy Superintendent." He has also received several awards: Superintendent to Watch (National School Public Relations Association, 2016), Champion for Youth (Mentors for Berks, 2017), Excellence in Educational Leadership (Boscov's, 2016), Courageous Institution Award (Mid-Atlantic Equity Consortium, 2017), Amigo Award (Daniel Torres Centro Hispano, 2017), Innovative School Leader (Pennsylvania School Boards Association, 2018), and the Jesse S. Heiges Distinguished Alumni Award (Shippensburg University, 2019).

EDUCATION

- University of Pennsylvania
- *Ed.D., Educational Leadership*
- Pennsylvania State University
- *M.Ed., Teaching and Curriculum*
- Shippensburg University of Pennsylvania
- *B.A., English*
- Northeastern Christian Junior College
- *A.A., Liberal Arts/English*

PROFESSIONAL EXPERIENCE

- **Superintendent of Schools**
- Reading School District
- Reading, Pennsylvania | 2014-Present
-
-

- **Superintendent of Schools**
- Caroline County Public Schools Denton, Maryland | 2011-2014
- **Director of Secondary Education**
- Centennial School District
- Warminster, PA | 2010- 2011
- **Middle School Principal**
- Klinger Middle School, Centennial School District
- Warminster, PA | 2006- 2010
- **Middle School Principal**
- New Hope-Solebury Middle School
- New Hope-Solebury School District | 2005-2006
- **Middle School Assistant Principal**
- Klinger Middle School
- Centennial School District
- Warminster, PA | 2003-2005
- **Middle School Dean of Students** Manheim Central Middle School Manheim Central School District Manheim, PA | 2001-2003
- **Seventh Grade Language Arts Teacher**
- Central York School District, York, PA | 1997-2001
- **Homebound School Instructor**
- Central York School District, York, PA | 1997-2001
- **Secondary English Teacher**
- Scotland School for Veterans Children Scotland, PA | 1996-1997

SOURCES|

(1954). Brown v. Board of Education, 347 U.S. 483
United States Supreme Court: 486.

(2012). Ending the School-to-Prison Pipeline.
<u>Subcommittee on Constitution, Civil Rights and
Human Rights of the Committee on the Judiciary United
States Senate</u> Washington, D.C.

Applied Research Center (2008). Historical Timeline of
Public Education in the US. Retrieved December 28,
2008 from <u>http://www.arc.org/content/view/100/53</u>

Baldwin, J. (1963). <u>The Fire Next Time</u>. U.S.A., Dial Press.

Barger, R.N. (2004). History of American Education Web
Project. Retrieved December 21, 2004
from <u>http://www.ux1.eiu.edu/%7Ecfrnb/index.html</u>

Bluestein, J. (1995). <u>Mentors, Masters and Mrs.
MacGregor</u>. Deerfield, FL, Health Communications, Inc.
Brown, B. (2015). The Legend Series.

Carreon, R. (2013). "Weber State Men's Basketball 50th
Anniversary Team." <u>Desert News</u>. from
<u>https://www.deseretnews.com/top/1366/5/</u>

DePasquale, P. A. G. E. (2018). Auditor General
DePasquale Calls Reading School District Turnaround
'Unprecedented'. Harrisburg, Pennsylvania: 1.

Dewey, J. (1916). Democracy and education. New York, The Free Press.

Drucker, P.F. (2006). Classic Drucker. Boston, Harvard Business School Publishing Corporation.

Echols, C. (2006). "Challenges facing black american principals: a conversation about coping." Retrieved February 10, 2007, 2007, from http://cnx.org/content/m13821/latest/.

Editors, B. c. (2014). Arthur Ashe Biography, A&E Television Networks.

Elizabeth Chuck, A. J. a. C. S. (2018). 17 killed in mass shooting at high school in Parkland, Florida: https://www.nbcnews.com/news/us-news/police-respond-shooting-parkland-florida-high-school-n848101.

Ellison, R. (1952). Invisible Man. U.S.A., Random House.

Elmore, R. F. (2002). "Hard questions about practice." Educational Leadership 59(8): 22-25.

Ford, P. (1983). "Philadelphia School Chief Submits Voluntary Desegregation Plan." Education Week 3(6).
Gordon, J. A. (2005). "In search of educators of color: If we make school a more positive experience for students of color, they'll be more likely to continue with their

education, and perhaps select teaching as a profession."
Leadership **35**(2): 30.

Green, R. L. (2014). Expect the Most Provide the Best.
U.S.A., Scholastic Inc.

Helton, G. (No Date). Curriculum Development in 20th
Century United States. Retrieved January 2, 2005 from
http://www.personal.kent.edu/~whelton/index.html.
The link is no longer active.

Hughes, L. (1994). The Collected Poems of Langston
Hughes. New York, Vintage Books.

J. Herrnstein, R. and C. A Murray (1994). The Bell Curve:
Intelligence and Class Structure in American Life.

Jensen, E. (2009). Teaching with Poverty In Mind.
Alexandria, VA, ASCD.

King, S. H. (1993). "The limited presence of African-
American teachers." Review of Educational Research
63(2): 115-149.

Kotter, J.P. (2014). Accelerate: XLR8. Boston, Harvard
Business School Publishing Corporation.

Kunjufu, J. (1991). "Countering the conspiracy to
destroy black boys." Black Collegian **21**(3): 170.

Larkin, R. W. (2009). "The Columbine Legacy: Rampage Shootings as Political Acts." **52**(9): 1309-1326.

Lloyd, J. W. (2005). Chronology of Some Important Events in the History of Learning Disabilities. Retrieved June 22, 2009 from http://faculty.virginia.edu/johnlloyd/edis511/classes/LD_Times.html.

Loehr, P. (1998, October 5). "The urgent need for minority teachers." Education Week: 32.

Lyons, C. A. (2010). "Burning Columbia Avenue: Black Christianity, Black Nationalism, and "Riot Liturgy" in the 1964 Philadelphia Race Riot." Pennsylvania History: A journal of Mid-Atlantic Studies **77**(3).

Maxwell, J. C. (2007). The 21 Irrefutable Laws of Leadership, Thomas Nelson.

Mumin, K. N. (2008). Effective Practices for Recruiting, Hiring, and Retaining African American Administrators in Suburban Public Schools: What Practitioners Say Works. Philadelphia, Pennsylvania, University of Pennsylvania: 165.

Pransky, K. and F. Bailey (2002/2003). "To meet your students where they are, first you have to find them: working with culturally and linguistically diverse at-risk students." The Reading Teacher **56**(4): 370-383.

Rippa, S. Alexander (1971). *Education in a Free Society, (2nd. Edition)*. New York: David McKay Company.

Russell, M. L. (2005). "Untapped talent and unlimited potential: african american students and the science pipeline." <u>Negro Educational Review</u> **56**(2/3): 167-182.

Santelices, V. and M. Wilson (2010). <u>Unfair Treatment? The Case of Freedle, the SAT, and the Standardization Approach to Differential Item Functioning</u>.

Sass, E. (2018). The American Educational History: A Timeline. <u>http://www.eds-resources.com/educationhistorytimeline.html</u>: <u>http://www.eds-resources.com/educationhistorytimeline.html</u>.

Sianjina, R. R., et al. (1997). "African-Americans' Participation in Teacher Education Programs." <u>The Educational Forum</u> **61**(1): 30-33.

Smith, D. (2017). Little Rock Nine: the day young students shattered racial segregation. Washington: <u>https://www.theguardian.com/world/2017/sep/2024/little-rock-arkansas-school-segregation-racism</u>.
Stankiewicz, M.A. (No Date). The History of Art Education Timeline. Retrieved June 22, 2009 from <u>http://www.personal.psu.edu/faculty/m/a/mas53/timelint.html</u>

Steve Vogel, S. H. a. D. A. F. (2012). Sandy Hook Elementary shooting leaves 28 dead, law enforcement sources say. Washington, D.C., The Washington Post: https://www.washingtonpost.com/politics/sandy-hook-elementary-school-shooting-leaves-students-staff-dead/2012/2012/2014/24334570-24334461e-24334511e24334572-24334578e24334570-e1993528222d_story.html?utm_term=.d1993529284fb1993528903f1993528225.

Thayer, V. T. (1965). Formative Ideas in American Education. New York: Dodd, Mead, and Company.

Walpole, M., et al. (2005). "This Test is Unfair: Urban African American and Latino High School Students' Perceptions of Standardized College Admission Tests." **40**(3): 321-349.

West, C. (1994). Race Matters. Boston, Beacon Press.

Zimmerman, E. O. K. A. S. (2007). Mosaic of Thought. Portsmouth, NH, Heinemann.